How to Open & Operate a Financially Successful

Painting, Faux Painting, or Mural Business

With Companion CD-R

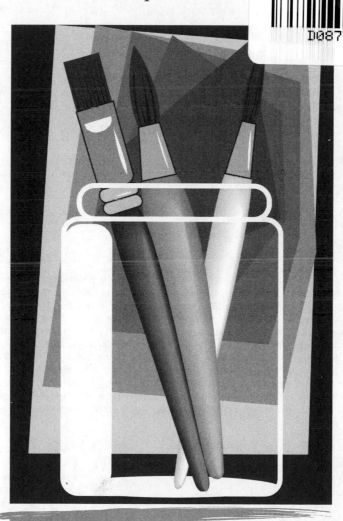

By Melissa Kay Bishop

How to Open & Operate a Financially Successful Painting, Faux Painting, or Mural Business: With Companion CD-ROM

Copyright © 2011 Atlantic Publishing Group, Inc.
1405 SW 6th Avenue • Ocala, Florida 34471 • Phone 800-814-1132 • Fax 352-622-1875
Web site: www.atlantic-pub.com • E-mail: sales@atlantic-pub.com
SAN Number: 268-1250

Library of Congress Cataloging-in-Publication Data

Bishop, Melissa Kay, 1971-
  How to open & operate a financially successful painting, faux painting, or mural business : with companion CD-ROM / by Melissa Kay Bishop.
     p. cm.
  Includes bibliographical references and index.
  ISBN-13: 978-1-60138-332-7 (alk. paper)
  ISBN-10: 1-60138-332-0 (alk. paper)
  1. Painting, Industrial--Management. 2. House painting--Management. 3. New business enter-prises--Management. 4. Texture painting. I. Title. II. Title: How to open and operate a financially successful painting, faux painting, or mural business.
  HD9716.P162B57 2010
  698'.1068--dc22
                                    2010042450

Printed in the United States

PROJECT MANAGER: Melissa Peterson • mpeterson@atlantic-pub.com
PROOFREADER: Hayley Love • hloveunlimited@gmail.com
INTERIOR LAYOUT: Dolores McElroy
COVER DESIGN: Meg Buchner • meg@megbuchner.com
BACK COVER DESIGN: Jackie Miller • millerjackiej@gmail.com
INSERT DESIGN: Jackie Miller • millerjackiej@gmail.com

Printed on Recycled Paper

We recently lost our beloved pet "Bear," who was not only our best and dearest friend but also the "Vice President of Sunshine" here at Atlantic Publishing. He did not receive a salary but worked tirelessly 24 hours a day to please his parents. Bear was a rescue dog that turned around and showered myself, my wife, Sherri, his grandparents Jean, Bob, and Nancy, and every person and animal he met (maybe not rabbits) with friendship and love. He made a lot of people smile every day.

We wanted you to know that a portion of the profits of this book will be donated to The Humane Society of the United States. *–Douglas & Sherri Brown*

The human-animal bond is as old as human history. We cherish our animal companions for their unconditional affection and acceptance. We feel a thrill when we glimpse wild creatures in their natural habitat or in our own backyard.

Unfortunately, the human-animal bond has at times been weakened. Humans have exploited some animal species to the point of extinction.

The Humane Society of the United States makes a difference in the lives of animals here at home and worldwide. The HSUS is dedicated to creating a world where our relationship with animals is guided by compassion. We seek a truly humane society in which animals are respected for their intrinsic value, and where the human-animal bond is strong.

Want to help animals? We have plenty of suggestions. Adopt a pet from a local shelter, join The Humane Society and be a part of our work to help companion animals and wildlife. You will be funding our educational, legislative, investigative, and outreach projects in the U.S. and across the globe.

Or perhaps you'd like to make a memorial donation in honor of a pet, friend, or relative? You can through our Kindred Spirits program. And if you'd like to contribute in a more structured way, our Planned Giving Office has suggestions about estate planning, annuities, and even gifts of stock that avoid capital gains taxes.

Maybe you have land that you would like to preserve as a lasting habitat for wildlife. Our Wildlife Land Trust can help you. Perhaps the land you want to share is a backyard—that's enough. Our Urban Wildlife Sanctuary Program will show you how to create a habitat for your wild neighbors.

So you see, it's easy to help animals. And The HSUS is here to help.

THE HUMANE SOCIETY
OF THE UNITED STATES.

2100 L Street NW • Washington, DC 20037 • 202-452-1100
www.hsus.org

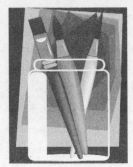

Author Dedication

This book is dedicated to all those who have a dream and are working toward making it come true. It is dedicated to those who are making the world a better place with their own special talents and creating happiness for themselves. Of course, it is dedicated to all who are painters at heart and those who are seeking a way to make their calling a way of life.

Table of Contents

Trompe l'oeil paintings in stairwell. Painting by Dan and Karen Dollahon.
Photo by Katie Sullivan.

Introduction

Every child is born into art. Shape, form, and color, mixed with imagination, capture the young spirit and mind, and thus begins a life-long relationship with art. However, at a certain point, many put away their paper and crayons and continue to simply live side-by-side with the art world. Whether it is the clothes they wear, ads they see, color of their walls, or trips to museums, art is still a part of their daily lives.

Others never closed the box of crayons. For these people, living alongside art is not enough and only fuels the need to make more of it. As we grow into adults, taking care of ourselves financially becomes the focus of our lives, but for many, that magical box of vibrant colors still calls. Luckily, for those compelled to heed the call, there is a way to answer and still make a profitable living. This avenue still lies in paint and color, but with a much larger work surface. By entering the painting, mural painting, or faux painting industry, the drawing tablet grows to the size of a house, a restaurant, or apartment complex.

By trading in the crayons or watercolor sets for gallons of paint, big brushes, and ladders, you can enter the home services industry, which according to the International Franchise Association, consumers in the United States spend $100 billion on each year. You can play with color and images while still paying your bills. This industry also allows for the freedom most artistic people enjoy by allowing you to create your own schedule and take on as much or as little work as you like.

If you have picked up this book, you are likely someone who has a box of paints tucked away or who keeps them out in the open and splattered on your clothes, proudly saying to the world, "I am a painter. Do you have any work for me?" I also suspect you have a desire to incorporate your life's passions into your life's work. With this book, I intend to help you do so.

Many of us with a proclivity toward art tend to be a little muddy on all the technical aspects of business. Although you would probably rather take an impressionistic approach to running your life and work, business is about coloring between the lines. This book will fill you in on all the details of business ownership with easy-to-follow tips, instructions, and examples. You will learn everything there is to know about being a successful, competent, and legal business owner and independent contractor. However, business itself does have a creative side that will allow plenty of room for your own personal touch and flair, to make it a creation all your own.

By reading this book, you will also gain insider tips on painting tricks of the trade from the experts. You will hear personal success stories from the pros and get advice on how to make your own success story.

Whether you are a doodler, hold a master's degree in fine art, or simply love the act of applying color to a blank wall, you will find valuable information in this book to help you take the leap from hobbyist to business owner. If you are undecided about whether you want to make that leap, this book will help you sort out all that is involved, giving you a solid place to land.

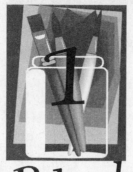

You, the Blank Canvas

> "For sheer excitement, you can keep movie premieres and roller coasters — an empty white canvas waiting to be filled, that's the thing."
>
> ~ Winston Churchill (1874-1965), Former Prime Minister of England

The beginning of any endeavor is like a blank canvas. The experienced painter knows the feeling of standing before a white space where there is endless possibility. This is where you begin and imagine where you might go. What will you create?

This is also where you stand before beginning a business and career as a painter. What do you want to create for yourself? Do you want to become a master of the art of painting? Do you want to create your own style that can be marketed? Do you want to do something you love while making some extra money? Or, do you want a full-time career as a muralist, faux painter, or interior painting business owner? Do you want to stay local or let your trade take you around the country or, possibly, the world? All these scenarios are possible when you take the right steps. Your career is your blank canvass. What will you fill it with?

A Portrait of the Past

The year was 17,000 B.C. The place was Lascaux, France. In a dark cave on the eve of man's transformation from Neanderthal to modern man, one man — perhaps considered a shaman within his society — communes with a blank wall. A rough stick in one hand, a plate of natural pigments in the other, he begins to invoke magic to bring about a successful hunt for his people. By rendering bulls, antelope, and other large animals on the walls of his home, his people believe he is capturing their spirit, thus securing the capture of their bodies for food, clothing, and basic survival.

This is a version of what happened at the first known painting site. Discovered in the 1940s by wandering teenagers, the cave in Lascaux, France is believed to be where the first mural was created. Because it is the first known painting, it illustrates that painting is a part of what makes us human and began on walls, not paper.

Painted walls are found throughout history. In Byzantine churches in Europe and Buddhist homes and temples in Asia, walls were painted and decorated by skilled artists. In America, the 1930s and 40s witnessed a surge of murals when the Work Projects Administration ordered the makeover of post offices and courthouses across the country, with images of historical and geographic significance painted on the walls.

Elaborate Chinese mural.

In the 21st century, artists are still working magic on walls of homes, churches, businesses, and government buildings. Transforming spaces with color and imagery has become the norm for any type of building.

Whether it is to warm up a space with an accent wall of a golden hue or create the image of a magical forest in the bedroom of a small child, painted walls are everywhere and come in many forms.

Painting Defined

Basic interior or exterior painting work can be found wherever there are buildings. Painters are highly sought after, especially where construction or restoration work is being completed. Even a simple coat of paint can transform a space. A gallon of plain white revives an old tired space into something fresh. Colors create specific moods for a room and serve as the foundation for its interior design. It is also the foundation for any mural or faux painting work.

Mural painting is defined by imagery. Scenes, portraits, or landscapes are usually the subject of murals. When thinking about murals, the image of a large wall covered with epic scenes and images comes to mind. But, a mural can also be a simple vignette or accent touch. Sometimes a wall calls for an isolated vine or branch to cut across an otherwise blank space.

"Faux" means "fake" in the French language. In painting, it indicates an image or texture that appears to be real, but is created with illusion and paint. Artists skilled in these techniques can turn drywall into wood, tile, crumbling brick, or mortar. Faux also includes accents that give texture to a wall with techniques such as graining or ragging. These accents are simple to learn. They are a matter of having the right tools and a little practice.

Faux painted copper door.

Another aspect of faux and mural painting is one that requires much skill and practice. As the French seem to have the market on painting

terms — it did originate in their country after all — the term trompe-l'oeil is French for "trick the eye." This technique is basedon illusion and creates images that are three dimensional and realistically rendered. The purpose of these images is to fool the viewer into believing they are not only looking at

Example of ragging technique. Painting by Gail Harrison.

paint, but an actual object. This approach extends to any object an artist can imagine. It can place stately columns in a simple home, floating flower petals on a wall, or even water drops on any surface.

A trompe-l'oeil of a classic style window, with a rough stone wainscot.

There is an ancient Greek tale that has been told throughout the ages about a contest between two painters. Zeuxis and Parrhasius, both born in the 400s B.C., challenged each other to a match of their skills. Legend tells that Zeuxis produced a still life so real that birds flew down from the sky to feed upon the trompe-l'oeil grapes. Parrhasius, in turn entered the room with a painting shrouded in tattered curtains. When Zeuxis tried to remove the curtains to see his opponent's contest entry, Parrhasius immediately won, for the tattered curtains were the painting itself.

Is Painting Your Passion?

Trompe l'oeil statue.
Painting by Dan and Karen Dollahon.

Zeuxis and Parrhasius obviously had a passion for painting. To produce works such as theirs, it takes a great deal of practice, which requires a love of painting. Owning a painting business also takes a great deal of passion, not only for paint and color but for creating something all your own.

If you are considering making your artistic calling your career, now is a good time to ask yourself some questions about your interest, drive, and determination to make your dreams a reality.

Consider the following questions:

1. Am I able to spend long periods of time enjoying the process of painting?

2. Does time seem to disappear when I paint?

3. Am I willing to constantly seek ways to improve my craft?

4. Do I enjoy the process of painting as much as the result?

5. Do I take great pride in what I create?

6. Am I happiest when I am in charge of a project and use my own ideas?

7. Am I physically able to paint for many hours?

8. Would I like a job where I get my hands dirty?

9. Am I excited about starting a project from scratch?

10. Do I know the limits of my technical skills and physical abilities?

11. Am I willing to make the effort to keep up with the many details that owning a business requires?

12. Do I keep my checkbook balanced?

13. Do I pay my taxes on time?

14. Can I keep my work area organized enough to suit my needs?

15. Do I love hunting for a bargain?

16. Am I comfortable negotiating prices?

17. Can I live comfortably without a regular paycheck while my business is in the beginning stages?

18. Am I good at working with people?

19. Do I receive a great amount of satisfaction by making others happy?

20. Is one of my goals to inspire others to succeed and be a role model?

21. Are my family and friends supportive of my business idea?

If you answered "Yes" to the majority of these questions, then becoming a professional painter might be the right path for you. While a love of painting is essential to starting this type of business, the requirements for becoming successful go beyond the enjoyment of creating color and imagery.

Painting is a very physical activity. Large amounts of time on your feet are required as well as having good upper body strength in order to lift a brush or roller repeatedly and carry ladders, gallons of paint, and

other heavy equipment. Keeping your body [...]
is recommended for this type of work.

It is said that a cluttered space creates a [...]
healthy mind and organized work area [...]
as a professional painter. Keeping t[...]
requirements requires self-discipline. As a pa[...]
keep your creativity flowing and problem-solving skills s[...]

As you might be beginning to realize, being a successful professional painter takes much more than putting color on a wall. If some of the tasks of running a business, such as bookkeeping and advertising, seem daunting, do not fear; this guide will walk you through all the fun — and not so fun — steps to success.

CASE STUDY: ART IS LIFE

Pablo Solomon
musee-solomon
Lampasas, Texas
www.pablosolomon.com
musee-solomon@earthlink.net

Pablo Solomon had a unique first exposure to art. When he was a child, the Southern Pacific Railroad was near his home. When muralists were hired to paint the station walls, Solomon watched the process.

After the project was complete, his father convinced the artists to give Solomon their leftover paint. His successful career as an artist began.

Solomon's art receives inspiration from life. He has traveled and experienced much. He takes in all the wonderful memories of people, places, and art. He claims all artists steal ideas and that if you study art long enough, you realize how little truly creative art is out there.

...s years of martial arts studies, he came to realize something ...ortant for an artist. You eventually understand that to truly be a ...r, you must develop a style that fits your body, your strengths and ...knesses, and your personality. Whatever you create must be based on ...awlessly executed technique, which then must be based on correct posture, breathing, timing, and focus. This is true in martial arts and visual arts.

Solomon said that art is his life. He often wonders if he could have done anything else, but always comes to the same conclusion: His path was planned before the sun was born. He said he has drifted from his path, run from his path, fallen from his path, tried to hack new paths, but always ended up an artist.

The best advice he can give is to learn all you can, experience all you can, work hard, live below your means, avoid losers, stay focused, stay positive, be thankful for life's blessings, and treat others with respect.

Always do your best. Even if your client does not know the difference, you will.

Experience: How Much You Need and How to Get It

"An artist's working life is marked by intensive appl cation and intense discipline."

~ John F. Kennedy (1917-1963), 35th President of the United States

For the advanced or aspiring painter, experience is essential. The more experience you have, the more confident you and your clients will be in your work. Building a portfolio of your best work will be key to showing off your experience, talents, and style. As you gain experience, document your work so you have proof of your skills.

Opportunities to gain experience are abundant and can begin on paper. As an artist, having a gallery of your art on canvas or paper can showcase your skills with color, form, and composition. This is the most accessible way to begin compiling a portfolio. You can use the walls within your own home to practice large-scale murals. If you do not own your home, check with your landlord first, and if you are free to color your walls, let your house become your canvas, portfolio, and advertisement. Be sure to put murals in noticeable places such as your entryway, so visitors will see them and have the opportunity to ask, "Who is your muralist?"

The best way to gain experience and market yourself as a great painter is through volunteer opportunities. A quick Internet search of the keywords painting, mural, volunteer, and the name of your area in a search engine can produce calls for help with beautifying an old building, school, or library. By joining a local network of artists in your area, you will receive notifications of these opportunities, as many people contact these groups when looking for help.

Education

Many artists gain experience through formal training. In higher education, there are degrees that a painter can work toward while building a portfolio. Many universities offer a bachelor's degree in fine art with a concentration in painting. These programs offer a well-rounded liberal arts degree with an intensive emphasis on turning the student into an artist. Other required courses such as photography, drawing, sculpture, and art history might accompany a painting degree. A degree in fine art is a full-time four-year degree. Obtaining a degree can also open other career opportunities in education or graphic design.

Each educational institute will have its own particular strengths, concentrations, and traditions. Some schools focus on abstract art while some promote realism or illustration. If you are considering a degree from a university, get a good idea of what type of classes it offers and the creative direction the classes take. Investigate the art professors and their styles of work. Attend student shows and talk to the students themselves. You would not want to have hopes of improving your photo-realism skills only to find your professor wants nothing but abstract work from you in his or her class.

Some of the top universities in the United States offering a degree in fine arts include:

- Maryland Institute College of Art (**www.mica.edu**): Located in Baltimore, Maryland, this college's tuition is $34,550 per year for out-of-state students and is known for its support of realism.

- Kansas City Art Institute (**www.kcai.edu**): Located in Kansas City, Missouri, famous names who call this school their alma mater include Walt Disney and Robert Rauschenberg. Out of state students pay $29,866 in tuition.

- School of the Art Institute of Chicago (**www.saic.edu**): Painting giants such as Georgia O'Keefe and Grant Wood attended this famous institute. Today, the yearly tuition is approximately $35,550.

- Memphis College of Art (**www.mca.edu**): Located in Memphis, Tennessee, this school is one of four independent, regionally, and nationally accredited art colleges in the south and the only school offering graduate degrees. Alumni go on to have careers as art directors, designers, and independent artists. Out of state tuition is $23,950.

- Massachusetts College of Art and Design (**www.massart. edu**): Located in Boston, Massachusetts, this is the first independent public college of art and the first to grant degrees. The school offers undergraduate programs in a variety of art concentrations including painting, animation, glass work, and metal smithing. Tuition for this school is $24,400 per year.

- College of Visual Arts (**www.cva.edu**): Located in St. Paul, Minnesota, tuition for this school is $23,448. It is a private four-year college offering fine art degrees with concentrations in drawing, painting, and interdisciplinary design studies.

- Columbus College of Art and Design (**www.ccad.edu**): Located in Columbus, Ohio, out of state tuition is $25,864 per year. This school's design programs include fashion, industrial, interior fine art, illustration, and media.

- California College of the Arts (**www.cca.edu**): Located in San Francisco, California, out of state tuition is $34,872. With campuses in San Francisco and Oakland, this college is noted for its interdisciplinary program. Famous alumni include ceramicist Robert Arneson.

- Maine College of Art (**www.meca.edu**): Located in Portland, Maine, tuition is $28,280 per year. This school offers a bachelor's and master's degree of fine art as well as continuing education classes for adults and youth.

- Savanna College of Art and Design (**www.scad.edu**): Located in Savannah, Georgia and known for its design program, this may be an ideal place for a mural or faux painter to study. It offers a full university experience in a liberal arts college that is focused on the visual arts. Tuition is $29,070 per year.

Community or private classes

A four-year degree takes time and quite a bit of money. If you are not able to make this type of investment, but would like professional help to improve your painting skills, there are other options for educating your inner artist.

Many community colleges offer a concentration in art. These programs extend up to two years to earn an associate degree and credits can be transferred to a four-year college or university to hieve a bachelor's degree. Tuition at a community college is usually much less expensive and the classes quite a bit smaller than at a large university.

If your local community college offers a concentration in art, classes will usually include introductory and intermediate classes in areas such as painting, drawing, or photography. In order to receive your associate degree, you will also need to take core classes such as English and math. If you are not looking to get your associate degree, you can simply take the art classes as a non-degree seeking student.

Taking art classes with your city or county parks and recreation department is also an option as well as seeking a private art teacher. To find a private teacher, visit your local art supply store, which should have a bulletin board where private teachers can advertise their services, or ask employees who work at the store if they know of any reputable private art teachers.

Taking art classes is a good idea for any artist. Whether you are a beginner or have been recreating the world through paint for years, classes are a valuable experience for artists. They not only provide the motivation to continue painting but also are an excellent way to receive feedback on your work from other artists. Classes are also a great place to create a network of artists who share ideas and build your portfolio.

Your Portfolio

A portfolio is a portrait of you as an artist and a professional. Unless clients are able to see work you have previously completed, they are not likely to grant you free reign on their walls. A good portfolio should be a collection of your best work. It should also show your range of style and subject matter. As an artist, your portfolio should include drawings of people, animals, flowers, buildings, cars, landscapes, preliminary mural sketches, and completed paintings on canvas or a wall. If you have examples of cartoon work and photo-realist paintings, include both in your portfolio. If you have painted a jungle scene with friendly animals for a child and an impressionistic landscape for an upscale restaurant, be sure to show each to your clients. The more diverse your portfolio is, the better the chances are that you will be a match for a client.

When meeting with a potential client, it is a good idea to have a hard copy of your portfolio. This should include printed images of your work in a binder or kept loosely in a professional portfolio case, which can be purchased at most art supplies stores. It is best to include only copies of your work in order to protect your originals and to keep your presentation of your smaller works consistent with the larger paintings that can only be presented by photograph in a binder. You should have a good camera to take quality photographs of your work for your portfolio and a color printer for printing the photographs. If you do not have a color printer or your printer does not produce quality photographs, your photos can be printed at any professional photo printer.

Including a résumé, references, and letters of recommendation in your portfolio are also a good idea. Include anything that will tell people you are a talented and reliable painter. Creativity is always allowed when making your portfolio, but be sure to keep it neat and professional.

Chapter 7 will discuss the importance of having your own website. Your business's website is a type of portfolio that will attract clients from afar and give them a chance to learn about you and your services.

As you create works of art, document all your best work. Whether it is something you made in a class, on the walls of your own home, through a volunteer opportunity, or for a paying job, it is essential that you have a record of your work. Documenting your talents will be the most valuable tool in securing future work.

Having a portfolio is a good idea for the basic interior painter as well. Your portfolio should show your ability to take on large-scale projects as well as your willingness to work smaller jobs. Potential clients will want to see that you have painting experience and that the result was attractive and tidy.

This is your beginning, your blank wall. Like the layering of colors to create the right hue, this business builds upon experiences and can evolve into a viable way to make a living

Priming Your Painting Business

"Don't judge each day by the harvest you reap, but by the seeds you plant."

~ Robert Louis Stevenson (1850–1894), *Author of Treasure Island*

Having an eye for color and a business mind-set are valuable tools for success in the painting business. Most likely, you already have a flair for color, but you might be in the dark about the concrete matters of business. It is time to think critically about what it takes to succeed. Some essential factors to long-term business success are:

1. **Passion.** A successful business is "more than a business" to its owner.

2. **Planning.** A solid business foundation is built on a well-considered strategic plan.

3. **Excellent customer relations.** This is the hallmark of success.

4. **Quality, reliability, and service.** These are the qualities that are emphasized to create a trustworthy reputation.

5. **Routine checkups.** Procedures, products, pricing, and all the strategic necessities of the business are regularly evaluated and monitored by the owner.

6. **Flexibility.** A flexible business remains successful as it adapts readily to changes in the industry, technology, and market.

Almost everyone has dreamed of owning his or her own business. Often, these dreams are the result of dealing with difficult bosses, low pay, long hours, swing shifts, and other frustrations that come with working for someone else. In the safe confines of the imagination, the vision of owning a business is immensely satisfying: You are your own boss, you make your own decisions, and you do not have to answer to anyone else. What could be better?

While there are elements of truth in this dream-world vision of business ownership, it is also true that, in reality, business owners have problems too. The problems are different from the frustrations faced by employees, but they are serious and stomach wrenching just the same. You will want to know your personal capacity to deal with the problems of business ownership before you jump out of the workforce and take over the boss's chair.

As the owner of your business, you will be the one held responsible for any property damages that might occur while you or your employees are at the work site. You will be the one held accountable to the government for paying your taxes on time. You will also be responsible for taking care of your own insurance and savings. As the owner and creator of your business, it will be your efforts and talents that will determine the revenue you generate and the success or failure of your venture.

Determine the Marketability of a Painting Business

You should first determine whether your painting business is going to make money and whether there is a market for it in your area. In almost every corner of the country, basic interior painting is needed, but how much depends on the amount of industry, development, or restoration occurring in the area. Decorative painters also need to seek areas with an affluent demographic. Decorative painting is a luxury that people will not spend money on unless they have the financial freedom to do so. You must next determine whether you can reach that market and how to do it.

A great clue as to whether a painting business is needed in a certain area will be if the population is growing or shrinking. Cities and towns that are experiencing population growth are also experiencing an increase in construction, the number of people moving into new homes, and the growth of new businesses. Painters will be in great demand for all of these categories. Right now, one of the best cities to start a painting business is New Orleans. The birthplace of jazz lost half of its population when Hurricane Katrina blew through in 2005. Now, the city is rebuilding, and many people are moving in. New Orleans is now the fastest growing city in the United States. Other cities experiencing a population boom are:

- New York, New York
- Phoenix, Arizona
- Houston, Texas
- Round Rock, Texas
- Cary, North Carolina
- Gilbert, Arizona
- McKinney, Texas

Due to new technology businesses that are springing up in the South and Northerners retiring and moving to warmer climates, the South and the West are experiencing the most growth and are great places to participate in helping people make themselves at home with a new paint job. You must have a way to market or advertise your business. If no one can find you or knows about you or your service, then you are not going find clients. Therefore, making sure that you thoroughly research the demographics and painting businesses already in the area is crucial. You do not want to start a business that is going to be impossible for you to market or advertise. A worst-case scenario would be trying to market a business that no one is interested in patronizing. This first step is going to save you from any of that.

An easy way to start your research is to do a basic search for painting businesses on an Internet search engine. Although the Internet is not always reliable and the information might need to be double-checked for accuracy, it is a good place to start. While conducting your search, you will also find any other businesses that might be similar to yours. If you search for other faux painters, you might also find interior painters, interior designers, and muralists. If this is the case, you can be fairly certain there is a market for you. Checking to see whether there are any publications, magazines, or newspapers that cover painting services will let you know whether there is a market as well. This is a good sign that you are on the right track and your business is marketable. If you find other muralists, find a unique quality to set yourself apart from the others; then, success could be yours. Your hallmark quality could be your unique painting style or the ability to find a specialty, such children's themes or recreating classics of painting masters.

You can also use a meta-search engine. This is a search engine that will incorporate results from more than one search engine at once. This is a good timesaver and is very effective. Dogpile (**www.dogpile.com**) and Clusty (**http://clusty.com**) are examples of meta-search engines.

Market area research

Wherever you decide to do business, you will need to research local demographics and market conditions. "Market" is one way of referring to a city or a metropolitan statistical area (MSA). MSA is a term used in census research and is an area with at least one major city that includes counties located within the MSA. Decide on a target city for your painting business and begin looking at various parts of the city. Focus on the parts that would be good for a painting business such as new areas where homes and businesses are being built or affluent neighborhoods where people can afford to hire muralists and faux painters.

Evaluate the following specifics about any location you are considering:

- How many painting businesses are located in the area?
- What is the average sales volume for a painting business in that area (check business licenses for previous year)?
- What is the population of the immediate area?
- Is the population increasing, stationary, or declining?
- Are the residents of all ages or old, middle-aged, or young?
- What is the average sales price and rental rates for area homes?
- What is the per capita income?
- What is the average family size?

Population and demographics

Population and demographics are factors to consider in choosing your location. The United States Census Bureau (**www.census.gov**) can supply important information and statistics about the interior painting industry.

Demographics to evaluate include:

- Population density
- Personal income
- Age groups
- Ethnic populations
- Employment statistics

An ideal demographic for a basic interior painting business is one with a high population density where people are gainfully employed and can afford to pay others to paint — rather than trying to do it themselves in order to save money. The majority of building structures have walls that can be painted, so where there are more buildings, there is more opportunity for work.

A decorative painter needs to seek a demographic with a high personal income. Placing yourself among people with money to spare is essential. Families struggling to put food on the table are going to cut out frills, such as having a Tuscan landscape painted in their dining room. Families with small children, however, are more likely to spend extra money to decorate bed and play rooms for their children.

A good source for information is the local chamber of commerce where you want to set up your business. A chamber of commerce is a form of business network or a local organization of businesses whose goal is to further the interests of businesses. Business owners in towns and cities form these local societies to advocate on behalf of the business community. Local businesses are members, and they elect a board of directors or executive council to set policy for the chamber. The board or council then hires a president, CEO, or executive director, plus staffing appropriate to size, to run the organization. To contact a chamber in another area, visit Chamber of Commerce.com (**www.chamberofcommerce.com**). At this website, you can get in touch with groups related to painting businesses, such as a local interior design association or art groups, and peers who can assist you with economic and lifestyle patterns for your business research.

Your library and online sources can provide valuable information. There are research librarians who can help you. Visit DemographicsNow (**www.demographicsnow.com**) to find out the market statistics in different areas of the United States.

The American Community Survey (**www.census.gov/acs**) provides additional information from the supplemental census survey. This information includes demographics by county and MSAs. The following are additional resources you can use to research demographic information:

- CenStats Databases (**http://censtats.census.gov**): This website provides economic and demographic information that you can compare by county. The information is updated every two years.
- County Business Patterns (**www.census.gov/econ/cbp/index.html**): Economic information is reported by industry, and the statistics are updated each year. Statistics include the number of establishments, employment, and payroll for more than 40,000 ZIP codes across the country. Metro Business Patterns provides the same data for MSAs.
- American FactFinder (**http://factfinder.census.gov**): Allows you to evaluate a wide variety of U.S. Census data.

CASE STUDY: OPERATING A BUSINESS IN A SMALL COMMUNITY

David Kinker
Freelance Artist/Muralist
www.kinker.com
kinker@bendbroadband.com

David Kinker is an accomplished artist among other things. He has a diverse background that he uses as a resource for his artistic insight and inspiration.

With a Bachelor of Arts degree in visual communications with an emphasis on illustration, he creates not only murals but also pieces of his own. He regularly shows them in regional galleries and businesses. However, his true passion is working as a freelance artist on commissioned murals and illustrations, of which he has done many.

Kinker has built his success on not only his talents, but by being an active member of his community. He said that as far as location goes, a larger city equals more opportunities; although, he lives in a small town where to be successful, diversity of abilities are required. He said that different opportunities for income from your skills and talents are more beneficial than the money you receive. Kinker said the best advertising for him is through the other artistic endeavors that he does. He said that in turn, each genre builds the other.

For Kinker, hand-painted signs, murals, illustrations, fine art, and art instruction make him increasingly successful. He said that building from the grass roots of a community has given him the luxury of a word-of-mouth business — like a painting that gets better as you add strokes.

Kinker supports and is involved in his community by creating murals in nursing homes, child care centers, and social service buildings. He also works with numerous non-profit organizations to produce decorative signs and illustrations helping to enhance their image.

When living in a smaller community, you have to be on the lookout for all opportunities. Kinker likes to touch base with new business owners. When a business is new, the excitement is high and this is when business owners want to make a big splash. Murals are a good solution.

Scouting the competition

Never underestimate the value of knowing your competition. Take a detailed look at your competition by making a list of the other painters and muralists in your area. Find out what other painters charge or what style or themes are present in their businesses. The information you need can be hard to find. The best way to discover information about your competition is to visit to its websites. This will give you an overview of what these businesses offer and what they charge. You can then ask yourself, "What can I do differently or better?"

Other sources of information on competition include:

- The telephone book. This will give you the number and location of your competitors.

- Your local chamber of commerce. This organization has lists of local businesses. Verify whether it is a complete list and not just chamber members.

- Local newspapers. Study the local advertisements and help wanted ads. There could also be a weekly home or lifestyle section with information about local painting businesses.

- Mark your proposed location on a street map. You can determine how far to research depending on how far you are willing to travel.

Once you determine your target area, look at every business that is similar to yours, and ask yourself the following questions:

- Was their advertisement informative and inviting?
- Does their website provide an extensive and professional portfolio?
- Do they provide any customer testimonials?
- Do they offer anything unique?

Once you have taken a good look at the competition, ask yourself what you could do different or better. Could you charge less? Could you offer a unique style or theme that is not already present? Or, could you do a specific style or theme better than what is currently offered in the area's industry? These are opportunities to set you apart rather than being lost among the competition.

Prepare a Business Plan

Once you get the inspiration to start a painting business, thoughts and ideas will begin bouncing around your head, and it is best to track and organize them. The best way to do this is to begin developing a business plan. Business plans are your roadmap to success. Preparing one will start the process of critically thinking about everything you need to cover in order to be successful. They also come in handy when you need to apply for a business loan. The only way you can reach your goal of operating a successful painting business is by having a plan. It is difficult at best to establish and operate a business when you do not quite know how to go about it — let alone when trying to accomplish it without a thorough assessment of your goals, how your plan achieves those goals, and what financial support you need to be successful. As you prepare to undertake the task of starting a painting business, evaluate your situation as it stands today and visualize where you want to be three to five years from now. In three years, you might see yourself having enough resources to take on a new client each month. In five years, you might envision the need to hire an employee.

To work your way from today's standpoint to owning and operating a successful business, you must set goals to reach along the way that will serve as benchmarks on your road to success. A business plan specific to a painting business will be included in the accompanying CD-ROM.

A business plan should:

- State your business goals
- Describe the approach you will take to accomplish those goals
- Discuss what potential problems you might encounter along the way and how you plan to address those problems
- Outline the organizational structure of the business (as it is today and how you plan it to be in the future)
- State the capital you will need to get it started and to keep it in operation

There are various formats and models available for developing business plans. There are even entire books devoted to guiding you through the development of a business plan. However, before you constrain yourself to any one business plan format, take into consideration that business plans should be as unique as the business for which it is being written. No two businesses are the same, and even though some basic similarities exist, each business is as individual and unique as its owner. Therefore, even though it is recommended that you follow the basic structure of commonly used templates, you should customize your business plan to fit your needs. Most likely, you will not need to set aside plans or money for finding a location in your business plan as a retail business would, as you will probably start your business by working from home. You will want to include your research on demographics and your projections for the future. There are a number of websites that provide you with a variety of samples and templates that can also be used as reference. These include Bplans.com (**www. bplans.com**) and PlanMagic (**www.planmagic.com**).

When writing your business plan, stay focused on its ultimate purpose and take into consideration the many reasons why the plan is being developed and its possible applications. For instance, if you do not have a loan proposal and decide that you need one, business plans are great supporting documentation to attach to a loan application. Plans are also used as a means of introducing your business to a new market or presenting your business to a prospective business partner or investor.

Parts of a Business Plan

To organize your thoughts in a way that will help you think about the details of your new venture, a business plan is usually broken down into sections. Each part of a plan should address the critical points of your business. The following sections discuss the parts of a business plan.

Cover page

The cover page should be evenly laid out, with all the information centered on the page. Always write the name of your company in all capital letters in the upper half of the page. Several line spaces down write the title "Business Plan." Last, write your company's address, the contact person's name (your name), and the current date. The cover page should look like the following example:

NAME OF COMPANY

Business Plan
Address
Contact Name
Date

Table of contents

The table of contents should list the main sections and subheadings that are in the body of your plan along with their page numbers. The table of contents should be well formatted, neat, and have a professional appearance.

MISSION STATEMENT

It is very important that you present your business and its purpose at the very beginning of your business plan. A mission statement is only as significant as you intend for it be. It can be written and then disregarded as unimportant. However, it should be written and ultimately used as a beacon to guide you in the right direction, where you intend your business to go. Your mission statement should discuss the purpose of your business, the services that you provide, and a statement regarding your company's attitude toward your employees and customers. A well-written mission statement can be as short as one paragraph but should not be longer than two.

For a basic interior and decorative painting business, you will want to address the painting needs of the population in your area. As a muralist, you might want to write about a specific customer base that you will be aiming for, such as children's rooms or stately homes that would benefit from grand classic painting.

EXECUTIVE SUMMARY

The executive summary should be about one to two pages in length and should actually be written last, as it is a summary of all the information you have included in the plan. It should address your intended market, the purpose of the business, where will it be located, and how it will be managed. Write the executive summary in such a way that it will prompt the reader to look deeper into the business plan. It is a good idea to discuss the various elements of your business plan in the order you address them in the rest of the document.

DESCRIPTION OF PROPOSED BUSINESS

In this section, you should describe in detail the purpose for which the business plan is being written. State what you intend to accomplish with the business plan. Describe your services and the role your business will play in the overall market. Explain what makes your painting business different from all the rest in the area. Clearly identify the goals and objectives of your business. The average length for the proposed business description section should be one to two pages.

MANAGEMENT AND STAFFING

Clearly identifying the management team and any other staff that are a part of the everyday operations of the business will strengthen your business viability by demonstrating that the business will be well managed. Keep in mind that a company's greatest asset is its employees. State who the owners of the business are, as well as other key employees with backgrounds in the interior painting industry. Identify the management you have on board, which might even include yourself, as well as any others you might need in the future to expand your business. For instance, you might be your only employee when your business first opens; however, in your plans for expansion, you might think about incorporating someone well-versed in interior design who will have experience working with other painters, insight on painting techniques, problem-solving skills, and connections with other people in the interior design business, which is an advantageous circle for a painter to be in. The management and staffing section of the plan could be as short as one paragraph, if you are the only employee, or it might be as long as one or two pages, depending on how many people you have and anticipate having as part of your staff.

MARKET ANALYSIS

If you are new to the industry, include information that you have acquired through your market research and data collection. Numerous sources of information are available, both online and through printed media, which can provide you with a wealth of knowledge about the painting industry. This process will add validity to your presentation, and you will be better prepared to answer any questions that may be presented to you when using your business plan to apply for a loan. Essential elements to include in this section include your target demographics and their possible needs, a description of your services, a discussion of your competition, and your planned strategy for approaching the market. The market analysis element of your business plan should be one of the most comprehensive sections of the plan, and it might be several pages long, depending on the number of services you plan to provide and the market you intend to cover. In particular, the Target Market portion of this section alone can easily be two to three pages in length.

Industry background

Focus on the segment of the market of which you will be a part. Include trends and statistics that reflect the direction of the market in your area and how you will fit into that movement. As a painter, you could discuss the fact that wallpaper began falling out of style in the late 1980s, and now, people tend to use paint to color their walls more frequently. Discuss major changes that have taken place in the industry recently that will affect how you will conduct business. Provide a general overview of your projected customer base. Great sources to research online are First Research (**www.firstresearch. com/industry**) or *Painting and Wallcovering Contractor (PWC)* (**www. pwc-magazine.com**). This publication addresses the current trends in this industry.

Target market

This is one of the largest sections of the business plan because it addresses key issues that determine the volume of sales and, ultimately, the revenue that you will be able to generate for your business. Demographics will be the key issue for any painting business as well as the amount of construction in the area. The target market is who your customer, or groups of customers, will be. By this point, you have already decided on the role you will take on, so it is a good idea to narrow down your proposed customer base to a reasonable volume. As an interior painter, you might want to just address the needs of new construction. If you are a decorative painter, you might focus on a hotspot retirement community or a new area filling up with young families. If you try to spread your possibilities too thin, you might be wasting your time on efforts that will not pay off and end up missing some real possibilities. Identify the characteristics of the principal market you intend to target, such as demographics, market trends, and geographic location of the market.

Discuss what resources you used to find the information you needed on your target market. Elaborate on the size of your primary target market — your potential customers — by indicating the possible number of prospective customers, what their purchasing tendencies are in relation to the product or services you anticipate providing, their geographical location, and the forecasted market growth for that particular market segment. Expand your discussion to include the avenues you will use to reach your market. Include whether you plan to use the Internet, printed media, trade shows, or another avenue. Trade shows are exhibitions organized with the purpose of providing a venue where companies can showcase their services. Explain the reasons why you feel confident that your company will be able to effectively compete in such a vast industry. Discuss your pricing strategies to be able to compete in the global market, such as discount structures in the form of bulk discounts or prompt payment discounts. Finally, you must address potential changes in trends that might favorably or negatively affect your target market.

Service description

Do not just describe your service — describe it as it will benefit or fill the needs of potential customers and center your attention on where you have a clear advantage. Elaborate on the services your business offers. For an interior or decorative painter, you might want to emphasize the professional touch you will bring to any job by describing your regard for customer needs and schedules and how you will leave a workspace immaculate and in order when you are finished. You might also want to address your desire to listen carefully to what customers want and to deliver beyond their expectations.

Market approach strategy

How do you anticipate entering such a vast market? Do you anticipate carving out a niche? Determining how to enter the market and what strategy to use will be critical for breaking into the market.

MARKETING STRATEGY

In order to operate a financially successful business, you must not only maintain a constant flow of income but also boost your profits by increased sales. The best way to accomplish this is through an effective marketing program, such as promoting your products and services by advertising, attending trade shows, and establishing a presence on the Internet. The marketing strategy element of the business plan identifies your current and potential customers, as well as the means you will use to advertise your business directly to them. The marketing strategy portion of your business plan is likely to be several pages long — at least three to four pages — depending on how much detail you include in the plan. For a large, well-established business, it would probably be more appropriate to prepare a separate marketing strategy plan; however, for the start-up company, it would be appropriate to include the marketing strategy plan as part of the business plan. Even as part of the business plan, the marketing strategy section should include the following elements: services, pricing strategy, sales/distribution plan, and advertising and promotions plan.

Services

This section will focus on the uniqueness of your services and how your potential customers will benefit from them. Describe in detail what your business provides, how the services are provided, and what makes you unique and different from other similar painting businesses. Address the benefits of using your services rather than those of your competitors.

Pricing strategy

The pricing strategy segment is about determining how to price your services in such a way that it will allow you to remain competitive, while you are still able to make a reasonable profit. You will be better off making a reasonable profit rather than pricing yourself out of the market and losing money by pricing your services too high. Therefore, you must take extreme care when pricing your services. The most effective method of doing this is by gauging your costs, estimating the tangible benefits to your customers, and making a comparison of your services and prices to similar ones on the market.

Consider setting your price by taking into consideration how much your supplies and services cost you and then adding a fair price to the services in order to make a profit on the job. When determining your cost of services, take into consideration all the costs involved such as the cost of labor and materials, selling costs, and administrative costs.

You should also address how the pricing of your services compares to your competitors. If your price is slightly higher than that of the competition, you need to justify the price and why customers would be willing to pay that price for your services. In addition, it is noteworthy to point out the return on investment (ROI) you anticipate being able to generate with that particular pricing strategy and within what specific timeframe. ROI is a ratio that compares the net benefits — in this case, your services — versus their total cost.

Sales

Now that you have determined how to price your services, it is time to think about how you are going to sell them. Describe the system you will use for billing your customers. Also, address which methods of payment will be acceptable from your customers, including credit terms and discounts.

Advertising and promotion

Discuss how you plan to advertise your products and services through market-specific channels, such as the Internet, advertisements, or solicitation. Promote your business to a specific market. Beyond having an online portfolio, list or describe where you plan to spend your advertising dollars and how much each promotion is likely to cost the business. Find out how much it will cost to place an ad in your local paper or magazine as well as one in the yellow pages and include the prices of each. Set aside a printing budget to make business cards and flyers that you can strategically place in paint supply stores or grocery stores with a bulletin board. Choose locations where you, through your research, believe will generate a customer base. Canvassing, or placing flyers on doors of the right neighborhoods, will also take up quite a bit of your paper and printing budget, but may turn out to be profitable in the end. One of your goals in this section is to break down what percentage of your advertising budget will be spent in which media. For instance, the cost of advertising through trade magazines, trade shows, and via an Internet site differs significantly and the return on your investment for each might not be worth what you spent. Therefore, it is wise to carefully evaluate your advertising and promotion plans before putting them into effect.

OPERATIONS

Under the operations section, all aspects of management operations and logistics services provided should be discussed. You will need to include where you will store your equipment such as ladders, buckets, and paints and how you will transport these supplies to the work site. Concentrate your discussion on how to improve resources in operations and production, which will facilitate the success of the company. Remember that all of the information outlined in this section needs to be backed by realistic numbers, such as cost of buildings, machinery, and equipment, as well as salaries and such.

Discuss the business's current and proposed location, describing in detail any existing facilities. Include a discussion of any equipment you currently have or require in order to expand. If you have employees, or anticipate having them, give a brief description of the tasks the employees will perform or other duties to be performed by the administration team.

STRENGTHS AND WEAKNESSES

As is the case in most industries, the competition in the painting industry is tough, with numerous business owners in the market competing for the same prospects. In this section of the plan, elaborate on the particulars of your business that have enabled you, and will continue to enable you, to be successful. Discuss those things that set you apart and give you an advantage over your competitors, such as your particular geographic location, a supplier you found overseas that manufactures painting supplies at a great rate, or your prior painting experience.

There are no strengths without weaknesses and, as hard as it might be to face and deal with those weaknesses that could be holding you back, addressing them will actually help you to either overcome them or deal with them more effectively. Remember that having weaknesses is not a problem only your business faces; your competitors have weaknesses to deal with as well. Some weaknesses you might be dealing with at the time you are writing the business plan might be due to inexperience and limited exposure to the market, both of which you can overcome. For each weakness you identify, you must discuss how you plan to overcome or eliminate it. Although important, discussing strengths and weaknesses should not take way from other focal points of the business plan. Therefore, keep this section relatively short and no more than one page in length.

FINANCIAL PROJECTIONS

Financial projections are normally derived from already existing historical financial information. Therefore, even though your goal in this section is to address financial projections for your business, you should include some historical financial data that will help support your projections. If you are preparing a business plan as part of your business start-up process, then historical financial data will obviously not be available and working with estimates based on other similar businesses' performance will be acceptable. If you are using the business plan as part of the application process for a loan, then be sure to match your financial projections to the loan amount you are requesting.

When developing financial projections, you must take into consideration every possible expense — expected and unexpected — yet be conservative in your revenues. It is not critical that your actual revenues exceed the estimated amount; however, it is not a good situation when expenses are more than expected. Your projections should be addressed for the next three to five years, breaking down each year with the following information: forecasted income statements, cash flow statements, balance sheets, and capital expenditure budgets. Due to the nature of this section, you can anticipate it taking up several pages of your business plan, as you might want to include some graphs, in addition to the budget forms, to depict the information more clearly.

CONCLUSION

The conclusion is the last written element of the business plan. Make use of this last opportunity to state your case wisely, highlighting key issues discussed in the plan. Then, wrap it up and close with a summary of your future plans for the expansion and progress of your business. Use language that will help the reader visualize what you will be able to accomplish and how successful your business will be, should you receive the support you are requesting.

Supporting Documents

Attaching supporting documentation to your business plan will certainly strengthen it and make it more valuable. However, do not over-burden it with too many attachments; finding a balance is important. Before you start attaching documents, ask yourself if that particular piece of information will better your plan; if the answer is no, then leave it out. Documents that you should attach include:

- Copies of your résumé
- Tax returns and personal financial statements for the last three years
- A copy of licenses, certifications, and other relevant legal documents
- A copy of the lease or purchase agreement if you are leasing or buying space
- Copies of letters of intent from suppliers (if applicable)

Franchises

Franchised businesses are individually owned businesses that are operated under the name and rules of a large chain, called the franchisor. The franchisor has perfected the successful path of running the business and has created a plan that the franchisees will implement in their business. Everything in a franchise is standardized, with an entire program designed for you from start to finish. There are a few franchised interior painting businesses — such as Five Star Painting (**www.fivestarpaintingfranchise.com**), Color World (**www. colorworldhousepainting.com**), or CertaPro (**www.certapro.com**). Franchising may be an option for someone seeking support but who is also able to make a much larger initial investment. Some franchises will require an initial investment that might include a franchise fee, additional working capital, marketing package, and equipment package. This can add up to approximately $100,000.

The franchisor is selling the franchisee the right to operate a business using the company's name, logo, reputation, and selling techniques. The franchisor might sell a franchisee "marketing rights" to certain parts of the country — by ZIP code, for example. This common practice eliminates competition among owners of the same franchise.

If you purchase a franchise, you will often pay a set sum of money to purchase the franchise and a percentage of gross sales on each sale you make. You might also be required to pay into a national marketing fund. The franchisor might require you to use certain vendors and purchase marketing materials from them. The franchisor is interested in brand consistency and image in the marketplace, and it might prefer that you use its marketing pieces, or at least follow their marketing standards and guidelines.

Finding a franchise

There are various ways to find franchise opportunities. You can search online for painting franchise businesses. Visit websites such as FranchiseOpportunities.com (**www.franchiseopportunities.com**), Franchise Gator (**www.franchisegator.com**), or Franchise Direct (**www. franchisedirect.com**) for information on franchised businesses and to search for painting companies. *Entrepreneur* magazine annually gives a list of the top 200 franchised businesses and has many advertisements by franchisors trying to sell franchises.

Other ways to research franchise opportunities include attending a franchise exposition or conference, where the franchisors will be set up in trade show format. To find expo dates near you, periodically visit your favorite search engine and type in "franchise expo" or "painting franchise expo." You can also look at trade magazines for the painting industry online, such as *Painting and Wallcovering Contractor (PWC)* (**www.pwc-magazine.com**).

Remember that salespeople at these expos are there to sell the franchise. Prepare yourself to attend the expo with your only goal being to ask questions and obtain information. Purchasing a business is a big decision, and you would not want to make a quick decision. To make the most of your expo experience, consider creating a list of questions such as the following:

- How long has the company been in business?

- How many franchisees does the company currently have? How many are in your area?

- Is the area you would be interested in available? If not, what areas are available?

- What are the costs, including the initial cost to purchase the franchise, the royalties, and the marketing fees?

- How do the royalty fees work, and how long do you pay them?

- Are the royalty fees a percentage of sales or a set fee?

- What is the marketing fee?

- What assistance will the franchisor give you if you purchase? Is the assistance given just during the start-up phase or on a consistent basis?

- How much control do you have as a franchisee on what you sell or how you run your business?

- Can you speak to an existing owner? What background information on the company can the franchisor give you? How long has the company been in operation? What is the profit margin on the branches in various locations?

Investigating the franchisor

Request a copy of the franchisor's disclosure document, and review it carefully. The Federal Trade Commission has specific requirements regarding companies selling franchised businesses, and they require that this document be given to you ten business days before you sign papers or pay any fees. This is done so you are not pressured into signing a contract and have plenty of time to review the document, talk with your attorney, and research the company and the specifics involved with the contract deal.

The disclosure document, called the Uniform Franchise Offering Circular (UFOC), is supplied to pre-qualified franchisees. They are available online, are typically about 50 pages long, and will include many details. Visit the North American Securities Administrators Association (NASAA) (**www.nasaa.org/content/Files/UniformFranchiseOfferingCircular.doc**) to view the entire document in Microsoft Word. NASAA is an International Investor Protection Organization. NASAA's form includes the following outline, and any UFOC should include this information:

- Franchisor name
- Business experience of key officials
- Litigation record
- Bankruptcy record
- Initial franchise fee
- Other fees
- Initial investment, including franchise fee, equipment, and any other costs
- Any requirements about where to purchase products and services
- Franchisee's obligations

- Franchisor's obligations
- Territories, including exclusivity and growth options
- Trademarks
- Patents, copyrights, and property information
- Obligation to participate in operating the business
- Restrictions on what franchisee may sell
- Contract renewal, termination and transfers, and dispute resolution
- Earnings claims — estimates of what the franchisee may earn
- List of all franchise outlets, with contact names and numbers
- Franchisor's audited financial statements
- Receipt — signed proof that prospective franchisee received UFOC
- Use of public figures — payment to celebrities or high-profile persons and/or their investment into the system

This document will give you a comprehensive overview of the business, its stability, and the expectations of franchise owners. Study the expectations carefully, as you will be bound by a legal contract to these terms.

Benefits of franchising

Making a larger initial investment into buying a franchise can give you a jump-start and have several benefits including:

- **Growth.** They have created name recognition, which may help you quickly grow your painting business. Being associated with a nationally recognized company might help when you talk to lenders for financing and suppliers for accounts.

- **Experience.** You will be able to draw on the franchisor's experience and knowledge.

- **Consumer recognition.** Brand awareness and name recognition with consumers might give you an edge and instant credibility.

- **Systems and marketing methods.** The painting company has designed a system that works and a marketing plan that they supply to you. You are not starting from scratch.

- **Buying power.** You likely gain the benefit of greater buying power due to agreements the franchisor has with suppliers.

- **Training and support.** The franchisor has proven techniques, and it is in its best interest to share these with you and train you to manage and promote the business. A good franchisor will be there to help you with all facets of the business.

- **National marketing.** You will reap the benefits of an ad that runs in a metropolitan magazine, for example, that you would not be able to afford as an independent firm. This also sends a message to your customers that you are large and established. However, you must do your own local marketing and promotions.

These "benefits" are not a guarantee that you will be successful; however, they will likely give you advantages over your competition.

Disadvantages of franchising

You will have to follow the company's rules, such as the policy on dress code, allotted sick days, or vehicle decor. You are not in complete control of your business. It will not be your name in the logo; it will be the franchised name. The following are other issues you will have to accept with a franchise:

- You will be required to follow their standardized procedures and policies, whether you agree with all of them or not.

- You will share a portion of your gross sales with the franchisor. It is usually a set percentage and is not based on your profit on a sale. This is an additional overhead cost that an independent competitor will not have, and you have to consider this cost of doing business in your margin; in some instances, you must consider whether this will make you less competitive in terms of pricing.

- You may be required to purchase specific items from the company. For example, if the company changes their name or logo, you will be required to purchase new letterhead, envelopes, business cards, and similar items.

- The franchisor might require that it approve all of your marketing, ads, promotions, and signs.

- It is possible that the contract will be written to benefit the franchisor. This contract might set high sales quotas, give the company the right to cancel your agreement based on their criteria of what an infringement is, limit your ability to sell your franchise, and otherwise represent its best interests over yours. In this instance, if you have issues or problems with the franchisor, it will have the upper hand in terms of power.

- You can lose your franchise for breaching the contract. It can decide not to renew your contract, and if it does renew your contract, it might have the right to charge a new percentage on the royalty rate, or there could be other requirements.

- The contract might allow them to audit your books at anytime and possibly at your expense.

Franchise financing

The International Franchise Association (**www.franchise.org**) lists more than 30 franchise lenders in their Franchise Opportunities Guide. Also, the U.S. Small Business Administration (SBA) (**www.sba. gov**) works with banks with guaranteed loan programs for start-up franchisees. Lenders have discovered the potential for growth and stability within the franchise market and are willing to look at financing these ventures.

Coloring Inside the Lines

Artists tend to be free thinkers and are used to coloring outside the lines. Although this mentality serves your creativity well, it will not serve you as a business owner. Owning a business means you must follow legal guidelines and stay within the lines of the law. Doing so will keep you out of trouble. It will also put your mind at ease because you will know you are following the rules and keeping your business legal. This chapter will help the creative mind think inside the box and be a guide to the more rigid part of owning a painting business.

Deciding which legal structure you would like to build your business under will be the backbone of your operation. The legal structure of your business will set the platform for your everyday operations, as it will influence the way you proceed with financial, tax, and legal issues — just to name a few. It will even play a part in how you name your company, as you will be adding Inc., Co., LLC, and such at the end of the name to specify which type of company you are. It will dictate which type of documents need to be filed with the different governmental agencies and the documentation you will need to make accessible for public scrutiny, as well as how you will actually operate your business. To assist you in determining how you want to operate, the following description of the different legal structures is provided, along with sample documents that you might need to file with state and federal agencies, depending on where you live.

Becoming a Small Business

You might be thinking, "I just want people to hire me to paint, not become a corporation." However, the truth is, as soon as you alone are paid to beautify a wall, you become a small business. A small business is a company with fewer than 500 employees. You will be joining more than 26 million other small businesses in the United States, according to the Small Business Administration. Small companies represent 99.7 percent of all employer firms in the country and contribute more than 45 percent of the total U.S. private payroll. More than half are home-based. Franchises make up 2 percent. Residential and commercial painting alone is a $22.5 billion-a-year industry.

Legal entity	Costs involved	Number of owners	Paper work	Tax implications	Liability issues
Sole Proprietorship	Local fees assessed for registering business; generally between $25 and $100	One	Local licenses and registrations; assumed name registration	Owner is responsible for all personal and business taxes	Owner is personally liable for all financial and legal transactions
Partnership	Local fees assessed for registering business; generally between $25 and $100	Two or more	Partnership agreement	Business income passes through to partners and is taxed at the individual level only	Partners are personally liable for all financial and legal transactions, including those of the other partners
LLC	Filing fees for articles of incorporation; generally between $100 and $800, depending on the state	One or more	Articles of organization; operating agreement	Business income passes through to owners and is taxed at the individual level only	Owners are protected from liability; company carries all liability regarding financial and legal transactions

Legal entity	Costs involved	Number of owners	Paper work	Tax implications	Liability issues
Corporation	Varies with each state, can range from $100 to $500	One or more; must designate directors and officers	Articles of incorporation to be filed with state; quarterly and annual report requirements; annual meeting reports	Corporation is taxed as a legal entity; income earned from business is taxed at individual level	Owners are protected from liability; company carries all liability regarding financial and legal transactions

Sole proprietorship

Sole proprietorship is the most prevalent type of legal structure adopted by start up or small businesses, and it is the easiest to put into operation. It is a type of business that is owned and operated by one owner, and it is not set up as any kind of corporation. Therefore, you will have absolute control of all operations. Under a sole proprietorship, you own 100 percent of the business, its assets, and its liabilities. Some of the disadvantages are that you are wholly responsible for securing any and all monetary backing, and you are ultimately responsible for any legal actions against your business. However, it has some great advantages, such as being relatively inexpensive to set up, and with the exception of a couple of extra tax forms, there is no requirement to file complicated tax returns in addition to your own. Also, as a sole proprietor, you can operate under your own name or you can choose to conduct business under a fictitious name. A fictitious business name, or assumed name, allows you to legally do business as a particular name at minimal cost and without having to create an entirely new business entity. Most business owners who start small begin their operations as sole proprietors. The muralist or faux artist is usually a one-person operation and the sole proprietor of the business. If you have a fellow artist that you would like to collaborate with, you might decide to open the business together and would then file as a general partnership.

General partnership

A partnership is almost as easy to establish as a sole proprietorship, with a few exceptions. In a partnership, all profits and losses are shared among the partners. In a partnership, not all partners necessarily have equal ownership of the business. Normally, the extent of financial contributions toward the business will determine the percentage of each partner's ownership. This percentage relates to sharing the organization's revenues as well as its financial and legal liabilities. One key difference between a partnership and a sole proprietorship is that the business does not cease to exist with the death of a partner. Under such circumstances, the deceased partner's share can either be taken over by a new partner or the partnership can be reorganized to accommodate the change.

Although not all entrepreneurs benefit from turning their sole proprietorship businesses to partnerships, some thrive when incorporating partners into the business. In such instances, the business benefits significantly from the knowledge and expertise each partner contributes toward the overall operation of the business. As your business grows, it might be advantageous for you to collaborate with someone who is knowledgeable about painting or business practices and will be able to contribute to the expansion of the operation. Sometimes, as a sole proprietorship grows, the needs of the company outgrow the knowledge and capabilities of the single owner, requiring the input of someone who has the knowledge and experience necessary to take the company to its next level. For example, a single interior painter may do very well accepting jobs in new construction sites, which are usually straightforward wall painting jobs. However, if you begin to accept more jobs that deal with restoration or renovation of older structures, it might be beneficial to collaborate with someone who has architectural or home repair experience. This could take your business to the level of an all-encompassing renovation service.

When establishing a partnership, it is in the best interest of all partners involved to have an attorney develop a partnership agreement. Partnership agreements are simple legal documents that normally include information, such as the name and purpose of the partnership, its legal address, how long the partnership is intended to last, and the names of the partners. It also addresses each partner's contribution, both professionally and financially, and how profits and losses will be distributed. A partnership agreement also needs to disclose how changes in the organization will be addressed, such as death of a partner, the addition of a new partner, or the selling of one partner's interest to another individual. The agreement must address how the assets and liabilities will be distributed should the partnership dissolve.

Limited liability company

A limited liability company (LLC), often wrongly referred to as limited liability corporation, is not quite a corporation; yet it is much more than a partnership. An LLC encompasses features found in the legal structure of corporations and partnerships, which allow the owners — called members in the case of an LLC — to enjoy the same liability protection of a corporation and the record-keeping flexibility of a partnership, such as not having to keep meeting minutes or records. In an LLC, the members are not personally liable for the debts incurred for and by the company, and profits can be distributed as deemed appropriate by its members. In addition, all expenses, losses, and profits of the company flow through the business to each member, who would ultimately pay either business taxes or personal taxes — and not both on the same income. When a business becomes a corporation, it has the option of becoming an LLC, which many choose to do to avoid double taxing on self-employment and the business itself. Some painting franchises fall under this category, such as Protect Painters Development, LLC.

LLCs are a comparatively recent type of legal structure, with the first one being established in Wyoming in 1977. It was not until 1988, when the Internal Revenue Service (IRS) ruled that the LLC business structure would be treated as a partnership for tax purposes, which other states followed by enacting their own statutes establishing the LLC form of business. These companies are now allowed in all 50 states, and although they are easier to establish than a corporation, it requires a little more legal paperwork than a sole proprietorship.

An LLC type of business organization would be most appropriate for a business that is not quite large enough to warrant assuming the expenses incurred in becoming a corporation or being responsible for the record keeping involved in operating as such. Yet, the extent of its operations requires a better legal and financial shelter for its members.

Regulations and procedures affecting the formation of LLCs differ from state to state, and they can be found on the Internet in your state's "corporations" section of the Secretary of State office website. A list of the states and the corresponding section of the Secretary of State's office that handles LLCs, corporations, and such is included in the Corporations section of this chapter. There are two main documents that are normally filed when establishing an LLC. One is an Operating Agreement, which addresses issues, such as the management and structure of the business, the distribution of profit and loss, the method of how members will vote, and how changes in the organizational structure will be handled. The Operating Agreement is not required by every state.

Articles of Organization, however, are required by every state, and the required form is generally available for download from your state's website. The purpose of the Articles of Organization is to legally establish your business by registering with your state. It must contain, at a minimum, the following information:

- The LLC's name and the address of the principal place of business

- The purpose of the LLC

- The name and address of the LLC's registered agent (the person who is authorized to physically accept delivery of legal documents for the company)

- The name of the manager or managing members of the company

- An effective date for the company and signature

For instance, Articles of Organization for an LLC filed in the state of Florida will look something like this:

ARTICLE I - Name

The name and purpose of the Limited Liability Company is:

Fictitious Name International Trading Company, LLC

Purpose: To conduct...

ARTICLE II - Address

The mailing address and street address of the principal office of the Limited Liability Company is:

Street Address:

> 1234 International Trade Drive
> Beautiful City, FL 33003

Mailing Address:

> P.O. Box 1235
> Beautiful City, FL 33003

ARTICLE III –

Registered Agent, Registered Office, and Registered Agent's Signature

The name and the Florida street address of the registered agent are:

John Doe
5678 New Company Lane
Beautiful City, FL 33003

Having been named as registered agent and to accept service of process for the above stated Limited Liability Company at the place designated in this certificate, I hereby accept the appointment as registered agent and agree to act in this capacity. I further agree to comply with the provisions of all statutes relating to the proper and complete performance of my duties, and I am familiar with and accept the obligations of my position as a registered agent as provided for in Chapter 608, Florida Statutes.

_____

Registered Agent's Signature

ARTICLE IV – Manager(s) or Managing Member(s)

Title	Name & Address

"MGR" = Manager
"MGRM" = Managing Member

MGR	Jane Doe 234 Manager Street Beautiful City, FL 33003
MGRM	Jim Unknown 789 Managing Member Drive Beautiful City, FL 33003

ARTICLE V – Effective Date

The effective date of this Florida Limited Liability Company shall be January 1, 2009.

REQUIRED SIGNATURE:

_____

Signature of a member or an authorized representative of a member.

Corporation

Owning a corporation is not an impossible goal for a painter. Two well-known interior painting corporations are Above All Painting and Service Painting Corporation. Both provide service in Florida. Who knows where your business will take you or how large it will grow? Your interior painting business might expand exponentially or you might invent the next greatest painting tool. Somewhere down the line, you might want or need to look into the possibility of forming a corporation — the most formal type of all the legal business structures discussed thus far in this book. A corporation can be established as a public or a private corporation. A public corporation, with which most of us are familiar, is owned by its shareholders — also known as stockholders — and is public because anyone can buy stocks in the company through public stock exchanges. Shareholders are owners of the corporation through the ownership of shares or stocks, which represent a financial interest in the company. Not all corporations start as corporations, selling shares in the open market. They might actually start as individually owned businesses that grow to the point where selling stocks in the open market is the most financially feasible business move. If your painting business begins to expand and you would benefit from investors to fund that expansion, you might want to consider opening your business to shareholders. However, openly trading your company's shares diminishes your control over it by spreading the decision-making to stockholders or shareholders and a board of directors. Some of the most familiar household names are Arthur Cole Painting Corporation and Bruin Painting Corporation.

A private corporation is owned and managed by a few individuals who are normally involved in the day-to-day decision-making and operations of the company. If your painting business is co-owned by other painters or an interior designer, you can become a corporation. If you own a relatively small business and wish to run it as a corporation, a private corporation legal structure would be the most beneficial form for you as a business owner because it allows you to stay closely involved in the operation and management. Even as your business grows, you can continue to operate as a private corporation. There are no rules requiring businesses to change to a public corporation once your business reaches a certain size. The key is in the retention of your ability to closely manage and operate the corporation.

Whether private or public, a corporation is its own legal entity capable of entering into binding contracts and being held directly liable in any legal issues. Its finances are not directly tied to anyone's personal finances, and taxes are addressed completely separately from its owners. These are only some of the many advantages to operating your business in the form of a corporation. However, forming a corporation is no easy task and not all business operations lend themselves to this type of setup. The process can be lengthy and put a strain on your budget due to all the legwork and legal paperwork involved. In addition to the start-up costs, there are additional on-going maintenance costs, as well as legal and financial reporting requirements not found in partnerships or sole proprietorships.

Sometimes, finding the correct office within the state government's structure that best applies to your needs can be a challenge. The same office might have a different name in different states. In this case, the name of the office that provides services to businesses and corporations may be called Division of Corporations in one state, Business Services in another, Business Formation and Registration in another, and so forth. Therefore, to save you time and frustration while trying to establish a business, the following is a shortcut to help you can reach the appropriate office for filing Articles of Incorporation without having to search though the maze of governmental agencies in your state:

STATE	SECRETARY OF STATE'S OFFICE (Specific division within)
Alabama	Corporations Division
Alaska	Corporations, Businesses, and Professional Licensing
Arizona	Corporation Commission
Arkansas	Business / Commercial Services
California	Business Portal
Colorado	Business Center
Connecticut	Commercial Recording Division
Delaware	Division of Corporations
Florida	Division of Corporations
Georgia	Corporations Division
Hawaii	Business Registration Division
Idaho	Business Entities Division
Illinois	Business Services Department
Indiana	Corporations Division

Iowa	Business Services Division
Kansas	Business Entities
Kentucky	Corporations
Louisiana	Corporations Section
Maine	Division of Corporations
Maryland	Secretary of State
Massachusetts	Corporations Division
Michigan	Business Portal
Minnesota	Business Services
Mississippi	Business Services
Missouri	Business Portal
Montana	Business Services
Nebraska	Business Services
Nevada	Commercial Recordings Division
New Hampshire	Corporation Division
New Jersey	Business Formation and Registration
New Mexico	Corporations Bureau
New York	Division of Corporations
North Carolina	Corporate Filings
North Dakota	Business registrations
Ohio	Business Services
Oklahoma	Business Filing Department
Oregon	Corporation Division
Pennsylvania	Corporation Bureau
Rhode Island	Corporations Division
South Carolina	Business Filings
South Dakota	Corporations
Tennessee	Division of Business Services
Texas	Corporations Section
Utah	Division of Corporations and Commercial Code
Vermont	Corporations

Virginia	Business Information Center
West Virginia	Business Organizations
Washington	Corporations
Washington, D.C.	Corporations Division
Wisconsin	Corporations
Wyoming	Corporations Division

S Corporation

An S Corporation is a form of legal structure; under IRS regulations designed for the small businesses, "S Corporation" means Small Business Corporation. Until the inception of the limited liability company form of business structure, forming S Corporations was the only choice available to small business owners that offered some form of limited liability protection from creditors, yet afforded them with the many benefits that a partnership provides. Operating under S Corporation status results in the company being taxed similarly to a partnership or sole proprietor, rather than being taxed like a corporation.

Operating under the S Corporation legal structure, the shareholders' taxes are directly impacted by the business's profit or loss. Any profits or losses the company might experience in any one year are passed through to the shareholders, who in turn must report them as part of their own income tax returns. According to the IRS, shareholders must pay taxes on the profits the business realized for that year in proportion to the stock they own.

In order to organize as an S Corporation and qualify as such under the IRS regulations, the following requirements must be met:

- The business cannot have more than 100 shareholders.

- Shareholders must be U.S. citizens or residents.

- All shareholders must approve operating under the S Corporation legal structure.

- It must be able to meet the requirements for an S Corporation the entire year.

Additionally, Form 253 "Election of Small Business Corporation," must be filed with the IRS within the first 75 days of the corporation's fiscal year.

Electing to operate under S Corporation status is not effective for every business; however, it has proven to be beneficial for a number of companies through many years of operation. Most S Corporations are small and tend to be known locally. Because of the significant role S Corporations play in the U.S. economy, the S Corporation Association of America was established in 1996 serving as a lobbying force in Washington to protect small and family-owned businesses from too much taxation and government mandates. Membership in the association is comprised of S Corporations, both big and small, from throughout the nation. This includes companies such as the Barker Company, a family-owned business that manufactures custom refrigerated and hot display cases for supermarkets and convenience stores based in Keosauqua, Iowa. Another example is the Sumner Group, headquartered in St. Louis, Missouri. The Sumner Group is one of the largest independently owned office equipment dealerships in the nation.

CASE STUDY: LEAVING A LEGACY

Ed Palubinskas
CEO of USA GRAPHICS, LLC
Greenwell Springs, Louisiana
www.usagraphics.com
ed@usagraphics.com

Ed Palubinskas, the main artist and CEO of USA GRAPHICS, LLC, is a fantastic example of how an artist can start small and grow to be a large business. This self-taught painter and former full-time basketball coach found a need in the decorative painting world and, therefore, found his niche. In the 1980s, he began to notice how bland sports facilities were, so he designed and sent flyers to a few area schools, offering his mural painting services to enhance the school gym. With this first step, Palubinskas changed the face of sports facilities all over the United States and abroad.

Palubinskas gets his artistic inspiration from, as he tells it, crazy people, fans, and spectators. He said that they want intimidation and to show the world that they are bigger and badder than their opponent. He said that is where all the money is. By starting small and growing big, Palubinskas can now generate $50,000 in two weeks by doing what he loves. He said it is a rather lucrative way to live like a basketball star, which he nearly is because he also has another business as a professional basketball shooting consultant.

Palubinskas is a very versatile photo-realist who loves the fact that artistic images can last for centuries and really leave a legacy. In 1972, Michelangelo opened his eyes to the fantastic human potential when he saw the Sistine Chapel when he was preparing to play in the 1972 Olympics on the basketball team. He said that he did not realize he would be doing the same thing until 15 years later. The only difference is that Michelangelo traveled by donkey, and Palubinskas flies in jets. He used a brush, and Palubinskas uses air. He spent most of his time on his back, and Palubinskas spends most of his time on his knees. Palubinskas thinks this potential is in all of us, when others say it is a talent.

He also makes use of the many airbrushes, touch up guns, and spray equipment available to create his style. He swears by these tools because they cover a large area in a short time, and it greatly resembles reality due to the atomization of paint. He likes that the result is not caked on like a roller or brush. He experiences more versatility with air. Palubinskas's advice to the beginner: "Find what your limits are and once you recognize those, then work hard on making that a strength."

Trademarks

A trademark is a word, symbol, phrase, sound, or smell that represents the product to the public. Many trademarked logos and symbols are widely recognized, such as the bear silhouette for Behr Paint or the red brush painting a red line with cut out stars for CertaPro Painters. Examples of trademarked sounds are the chimes for the broadcast station NBC and the Yahoo! Yodel, and perfume scents are examples of trademarked smells. Your brand name, logo, or other symbol(s) differentiate your product from a competitor's. To be protected, the mark must either be used in commerce or registered with the intent to use it. While use in commerce is sufficient to establish trademark rights, registration with the USPTO can strengthen trademark enforcement efforts. The letters TM in superscript next to a word, brand, or logo used in commerce is sufficient to designate that the word, brand, or logo is trademarked. The "TM" symbol is the designation for a non-registered trademark. A trademark that has been registered with the U.S. Patent and Trademark Office (USPTO) is designated with the R with a circle around it — ®. Use of the registered symbol for a nonregistered trademark could interfere with the right of an inventor to subsequently register the mark. If you were to name your business, "Mary's Magical Murals" and design a logo of a fairy holding a paintbrush, you would not want another painter named Mary who likes fairies to do the same. You would also not want to unknowingly copy a business name and logo that is already being used. Just as a patent cannot be issued if the invention infringes on an already protected product, a trademark cannot be registered and will not have legal protection in court if it is not unique. While you know enough not to use UPS or Nike as your brand name, who knows if there is already a "Mary's Magical Murals?" The only way to find out is to search.

Trademark searches can be done professionally for between $300 and $1,200. Nevertheless, you can avoid these charges by using the Internet. Search registered and pending trademarks on the USPTO website (**www. uspto.gov**) and use the Trademark Electronic Search System (TESS). Go to the New User Form Search, type in the name you want to use, and click "Search Term." Be certain that the "Field" term is on "Combined Word Mark." To make sure that your search is comprehensive, be certain to perform the following:

- Enter all phonetically similar names of your company because names that are phonetically similar can cause conflicts in trademark use. For example, if you want to name your company Netflicks, you should enter Netflix as well.

- Enter the singular and the plural of your company's proposed name.

- If your proposed name has more than one word, enter each word separately.

- Use "wild card" search terms, such as the asterisk (*), to broaden your search. For example, if you are searching for Netflicks, you can enter Netfli*, to search for similar names that began with the same six letters.

Be advised that trademark searches are not foolproof. Searches reveal only those names that are registered. There may be unregistered business names that are in use as well. They would be considered valid even if they may not have shown up in the USPTO database. Consequently, after searching there, you should search the Internet for the proposed name. This would probably reveal any current users of your proposed name. If you have reached this stage without discovering any conflicting trademarks or service marks, you should then search the secretary of state's records for existing corporate names. Most states offer free searches of existing corporate names, generally through their Office of the Secretary of State.

If your name passes the previous tests, you might want to reserve it. This step is not absolutely necessary, but it is recommended as you move to the planning and development stages of your new business. Most states offer a reservation service where you file a short name reservation form with the secretary of state, but a fee is charged for this service, which will vary with each state. When you have finalized your name, if you have decided to incorporate your business, make sure that you have an appropriate corporate suffix to make the public aware of your limited liability protection. Include:

- Corporation or Corp.

- Incorporated or Inc.

- Limited or Ltd.; in some states, this suffix can be confused with a "limited partnership" or "limited liability corporation."

You can register a trademark with the USPTO prior to use in commerce, thereby establishing priority for the mark, if you plan to use the trademark in commerce relatively soon. Initial registration is good for six months and can be extended (for a fee) for up to three years. If the trademark is not used before the intent-to-use registration expires, the trademark is considered abandoned. It then becomes public and available for others to adopt.

Trademark protection

To be protected, the mark must either be used in trade or registered with the intent to use it. While use in commerce is sufficient to establish trademark rights, registration with the USPTO can strengthen trademark enforcement efforts. Because there is no test or evaluation for a trademark other than that it is used in commerce, a trademark owner will not know for sure the strength of their claim to their mark unless it is tested in court.

The criterion for evaluating the strength of an owner's claim to a mark is distinctiveness. If your graphic artist has devised an effective logo that does not resemble the logo for any other known product, certainly not a product in your industry — think of the bear silhouette for Behr Paints — then it is distinctive.

The more generic the name of your product, brand, or company, the less distinctive it is. If your mark is not protectable because it is generic or might only merit weak protection because it is solely descriptive, you might not want to bother searching to see if anyone else is using it. You likely could not prevail in suing them for infringement, and the other business likely could not prevail in suing you. If you think your mark is distinctive, then make sure no one else is using it in the United States, or at least in your service area, before putting it into use.

There are some things a mark cannot do. A mark cannot be a generic term; for example, you cannot trademark the name "Murals." A mark also cannot be a last name, use deception, include swear words or pornography, replicate the insignia of another party, include criticism of other people or organizations, or use a person's image without his or her permission.

Some marks that would be ineligible for protection when first put into use can become eligible for protection if they start acquiring recognition in association with your product. For example, Mary's Magical Murals might have little claim to protection when it first hits the market, but it might gain protection over time as its customers associate the qualities of the product with the mark. Marks that are initially entitled to protection can also lose that status if the name becomes too generic and the owners do not actively protect their trademark. "Laundromat" and "escalator" are two examples of former trademarks turned generics.

Fictitious Name Registration

If your business name is different than your real name, most states require that you file a fictitious name registration, "doing business as" (DBA) registration, or some form of similar registration that specifies that the name you are using to conduct business is not your own. If your real name is Mary Patterson and your business is named Mary's Magical Murals, then you will need to register for a fictitious name. The agency with which the fictitious name or DBA name is filed varies from state to state. In some states, the registration is completed with the city or county in which the company has its principal place of business. However, the majority requires the registration to be filed with the state's Secretary of State office. Of all 50 states, the only ones that specifically do not require any type of filing when conducting business with a name other than your personal name are Alabama, Arizona, Kansas, Mississippi, New Mexico, and South Carolina. Washington, D.C. makes it optional, and Tennessee does not require such filing for sole proprietorships or general partnerships.

Obtain an Employer Identification Number

All employers, partnerships, and corporations must have an employer identification number (EIN), also known as a federal tax identification number. You must obtain your EIN from the IRS before you conduct any business transactions or hire any employees. The IRS uses the EIN to identify the tax accounts of employers, certain sole proprietorships, corporations, and partnerships. The EIN is used on all tax forms and other licenses. To obtain one of these, fill out Form 55-4, obtainable from the IRS at **www.irs.gov/businesses/small** and click "Small Business Forms and Publications." There is no charge. If you are in a hurry to get your number, you can receive an EIN by telephone by calling the IRS at 1-800-829-4933.

You should also request the following publications, or you can download them via the Internet on the IRS website (**www.irs.gov**):

- Publication #15, circular "Employer's Tax Guide."
- Several copies of Form W-4, "Employer Withholding Allowance Certificate." Each new employee must fill out one of these forms.
- Publication 334, "Tax Guide for Small Businesses."
- Request free copies of "All about OSHA" and "OSHA. Handbook for Small Businesses." Depending on the number of employees you have, you will be subject to certain regulations from this agency. Their address is OSHA, U.S. Department of Labor, Washington, D.C. 20210, or you can find it online at **www.osha.gov**.
- Request a free copy of "Handy Reference Guide to the Fair

Labor Act." Contact: Department of Labor, Washington, D.C. 20210, or you can find it online at **www.dol.gov**.

The IRS has developed a website called the Small Business Resource Guide, which has been specifically designed to better assist the small business owner and those who are just starting their new business venture. This guide can be accessed online at **www.irs.gov**. Through this website, new business owners can access and download any number of the necessary forms and publications required by the IRS.

Open a Bank Account

Establishing a strong working relationship from the very beginning with a well-established financial institution is essential in ensuring your financial success. When you are starting a business venture, it is sound practice to seek the advice of business professionals in their fields of expertise, such as in the banking industry. Taking the time to meet with a bank representative when you open a business checking account is time well spent, and you will be surprised as to the many services available and the sound financial advice you can receive from bank officials. Discuss with a representative where you foresee your business going in the future. This information will allow the bank representative to better advise you as to which type of business checking account will best suit your needs. He or she can also provide you with information regarding services provided by the bank, which could benefit you during the early stages of your business and in the future. This is also a good time to find out about the bank's policy on a business line of credit account, which is beneficial to have when starting a new venture. A line of credit account is an arrangement through a financial institution whereby the bank extends a specified amount of unsecured credit to the borrower.

In order to establish a business checking account, most financial institutions will require a copy of the state's certificate of fictitious name filing from a partnership or sole proprietor or an affidavit to that effect. An affidavit is a written declaration sworn to be true and made under oath before someone legally authorized to administer an oath. To open a business checking account for a corporation, most banks will require a copy of the Articles of Incorporation, an affidavit attesting to the actual existence of the company, and the EIN acquired from the IRS.

Permits and Licenses

When advertising your painting business and seeking potential clients, it is always more impressive if you can state that you are insured and licensed. It displays professionalism and can instill a sense of trust in the consumer. Being licensed might also be legally required depending on your state and local laws. The following sections are an overview of what you will need and what will be expected of you as a painting business owner.

Contractor's license

Whether you are a decorative painter or an interior painter, you will need a contractor's license. The requirements to obtain such a license vary from state to state. Some states, such as California, require that you take and pass a painting and decorating exam. It is a multiple-choice exam that will test your knowledge of the essentials to painting. It is broken down into the following six parts:

1. Painting Project Planning or Estimation
    -   Assessment of job site conditions

- Materials selection
- Materials calculation
- Equipment and tools

2. Minor Demolition and Repair

- Causes of paint failure
- Substrate repair
- Removal of wall coverings

3. Surface Preparation

- Site protection
- Preparation of sound surfaces
- Preparation of contaminated surfaces
- Preparation of failed coatings
- Preparation of surface for wall coverings
- Pressure washing
- Repair of holes and cracks

4. Paint Application

- Application of primers
- Application of finishes
- Application of specialty coatings

5. Wood Staining and Finishing

- Exterior surfaces
- Interior surfaces
- Refinishing

6. Safety

- Hazard identification
- Elevated work

- Personal protection
- Waste disposal

Whether the state you live in requires such an exam, these are all aspects of the business that a painter should understand. To find guidance in these matters, a good place to start is with the Painting and Decorating Contractors of America. They offer manuals and textbooks and can be reached at 1-800-332-7322, or you can visit their website at **www.pdca. org**, where you can find information and locate a chapter near you.

City business license

You will almost certainly need a city business license if you are operating within a city, and you might need a county permit if not located within city boundaries. You can find out more about which licenses and permits you might need, where to get them, and how much they will cost by calling your city hall or county clerk's office. In most cities, the city clerk does not issue business licenses, but can direct you to the correct office if you cannot find it on your own.

You need a city license for several reasons, starting with the fact that you can be fined heavily for running a business without the correct permit. Most states will punish you with a fine of $500 and possible jail time of up to 30 days. You also need to show your customers that you are legitimate, and you will need a city business license in most states to get your sales tax permit.

When you contact the agency that issues the city business license, ask how long the license is good for, what the renewal process is, whether there are levels of licensing and what level you need, how much it will cost, and whether there is anything else you need to do to legally operate a business within your city or county.

State sales tax permit

Anything you actually sell, such as your painting services, will be subject to sales tax, and you could end up with a hefty fine for not reporting and paying sales tax as required by your state.

You can contact your Secretary of State's office to apply for your sales tax permit. You will need, in most states, a local business license to do this. Make sure you allow time to get your city license and sales tax permit before you open shop. Ask the agency issuing the permit whether it needs to be renewed annually, how to do that, how and where to file and pay sales taxes, and whether you need to know anything else in order to meet your obligations to the state regarding sales taxes.

In some states, it may be difficult to find information on the Internet about exactly how to apply for your sales tax permit. Calling or sending a written request for information to your state's Department of Revenue might be the best route to obtain the information you need.

State and county permits/licenses

Depending on where you live, state or county permits or licenses might be required to start a business. You should call your Secretary of State's and your county clerk's office to ensure you are not missing anything you need to apply for.

Plagiarism

As a muralist, you will often encounter clients who would like a recreation of art that already exists. Children might want a cartoon character-themed bedroom or an Italian restaurant may want a replica of the Mona Lisa on the wall. In all likelihood, you can give the client what he or she wants without worrying about copyright abuse; however, there is always a chance you could get into legal complications for using someone's art without permission. Because the object of this chapter is to keep you out of legal trouble, let's go over the finer points of copyright and plagiarism.

You are free to recreate the Mona Lisa because it is considered public domain. Any art published before 1923 in the United States or before 1909 outside the Untied States is available for public use. Art can be copyrighted by being published, and it is considered published once it is distributed, put up for sale, or printed in magazines, postcards, or books. Publication is not necessary for copyright protection and being registered through the Library of Congress gives a work copyright protection.

Part of a larger underwater child's mural. Painting depicts Sebastian from Disney's "The Little Mermaid." Painting by Ed Palubinskas.

On the other hand, cartoon characters are new and copyrighted, so you will need to get permission if you are looking to make a profit from the material. Whether you profit from using someone else's art or not, using copyrighted work is similar to using another person's property. You would not take your neighbor's car for a spin around the block without permission because it is illegal to do so — the same rules apply to using your fellow artists' work.

The first step is to find out who owns the copyright to this image. Sometimes the owner is listed along with the copyright notice. For example, Viacom International Inc. owns SpongeBob SquarePants. Contact information for companies is usually found on their official website, which can be found with a quick keyword search using an Internet search engine. Depending on your project and the temperament of the owner of the art, permission is frequently granted. If it is, you will probably be required to pay a fee, of which the amount will also depend on the temperament of the owner, for the image's use. Fees are often adjusted according to what you are planning to do with the image. If you will be using SpongeBob imagery for a volunteer project to beautify a community center, the fee will likely be lower than if you were going to use it for a private bedroom. The owner of the image should provide permission to use the image in writing. Failure to follow the proper steps in obtaining permission could result in court fees, and you could be fined up to $350,000, depending on the determined amount of damages the infringement caused.

On the U.S. Copyright Office's website (**www.copyright.gov**), you can search records to determine who owns artwork. You should also visit this site if you are interested in copyrighting your own artwork. You can protect your creation from legally being used by others by registering it through the Library of Congress. To register your artwork, you will need a quality photograph of the work. You can register the work in several ways, including:

- **Online.** This is the fastest way to register and the least expensive. The fee is $35.

- **Fill in CO Barcode Form.** This method involves completing a form on your computer, printing it out, and mailing it in with a $50 check.

- **Registration paper forms.** This tends to be the slowest process and costs $65. By visiting the Copyright Office's website, you can fill out your information by clicking "upon request" under this section. Forms will be sent to you by mail. Please note that the Copyright Office is trying to phase out this method of registration.

The Copyright Office's website is full of information to guide you through many aspects relating to copyright. For further assistance, you can call U.S. Copyright Office at 1-202-707-3000.

Taxes

Taxes are a critical factor in sound money management. It is essential to maintain records of all sales and expenses, down to the last penny. The IRS will want to see what money came in and what went out, especially if your business is ever audited. Clear, up-to-date records show that you are a responsible taxpayer and help avoid any suspicion of shady policies. Keep your company financially transparent to the parties that have a legal right to see the numbers. Keep careful records of any exchange of money between you and clients to show your income and receipts of your expenditures on supplies and all business related matters that could help with tax write-offs.

You should also recognize that keeping accurate books is not a favor to the government. Your financial records are an ongoing map of your business's life. If you do not keep accurate and detailed numbers, you will not have any idea how your company is doing financially. You must have the numbers and understand them to know whether you are meeting your goals and have a decent profit margin.

You will want to make sure your federal, state, and local taxes are filed on a timely basis. In some places, you might be required to collect sales tax on products or services, and periodically pay it to the governing body. Verify these requirements by contacting your city or state tax department. They will tell you what licenses or tax filings are necessary, as well as the schedule and appropriate ways to file. Many taxing entities are converting to online tax filings for businesses. You will need to set up a special account on the related government website to use online filing and payment method. For more information, visit the IRS website at **www.irs.gov/businesses/ small/index.html**.

Sketching Out an Insurance Plan

Insurance is a necessary expense, and in some jurisdictions, an absolute requirement for doing business. No matter how careful you are, accidents will happen — insurance is your protection. Many painters get by with simple liability coverage in case they should damage a client's property while on the job. Some feel better extending their coverage to workers' compensation, bonding, criminal insurance, or even business interruption insurance, especially as their business grows. As your business becomes large and successful, or if you grow to the point of hiring employees, then other types of coverage will be needed. We will discuss the various types of insurance that you might need now or in the future.

Types of insurance

Insurance is not a one-size-fits-all solution. Laws vary by state, so some states will have higher premiums, based on a number of factors, including the number of claims filed overall. Many states have minimum business insurance standards. Painting businesses usually cover themselves with liability to cover any property damage that might occur when working on and with a client's property. It is the nature of the painting business to work with these risks. If you hire employees, you should also pay into worker's compensation coverage, because with physical work, especially that which requires climbing on ladders, there is a risk of injury. If a painting business grows exponentially or is a franchise, other types of insurance may be needed.

Comprehensive general liability insurance

General liability insurance might be required in your state. This type of insurance will cover your business against unexpected accidents and injuries. With a painting business, you run the risk of you or your employees falling off ladders or breaking a client's furniture or valuables while on the work site. Review the policy for exclusions that might leave you vulnerable to exposure under certain circumstances. Read the fine print — do not ignore it or skim over it. For example, if your policy excludes damage caused by drunken employees, the insurance company might not help you if an inebriated employee loses control of your company truck.

Know what you need and what coverage an insurance company is providing. Talk to a number of providers. Better yet, ask other business owners for referrals to reputable insurance brokers who deal with a range of insurance companies. He or she will shop around for the coverage you need at the lowest cost. The most important part of this process is obtaining the proper coverage. A lower premium is not worth much if you find yourself without the insurance protection you need. Look at the areas that you expect to work in. Do you expect to be in mansions that will have expensive valuables? Although such items should be removed from the working area by the owner prior to your arrival, you will be carrying equipment such as ladders and paint through their home and the unforeseen might occur.

How much liability coverage is enough? $1 million sounds like a lot, but in today's world, this amount might not be enough. A good minimum is probably $2 million, and $3 million is even safer. If you can afford it, go higher. You will find that insurance companies price this type of insurance reasonably, assuming you do not have a history of claims and judgments, and premiums are not based on a dollar-for-dollar fee schedule. For example, $2 million in coverage is less than twice the cost of $1 million and so on. An insurance broker who specializes in small business coverage can help you determine what you need. Be honest with him or her, and do not mislead the broker, or yourself, about what you will be doing in your business. Ask questions, write down the coverage you need and any promises regarding coverage from the provider or the broker, and check these items against the actual insurance policy.

Workers' compensation insurance

Workers' compensation is required in every state; however, the structure of the insurance varies by state. Workers' compensation is a form of insurance that provides compensated medical care for employees who are injured in the course of employment, in exchange for mandatory relinquishment of the employee's right to sue his or her employer for negligence. Private insurance companies offer this coverage based on the number of employees on the payroll, the roles each individual performs, and the type of business you are operating. The premiums for workers' compensation coverage are based on your payroll. However, some states require that such coverage be obtained from the state government or one of its agencies. Workers' compensation pays medical expenses and lost wages for workers who are injured on the job. There are exclusions for certain categories, such as independent contractors and volunteers, but check your state's laws. Check with your state's Department of Labor to find out more. Business owners are generally exempt in most cases.

Bonding

If you already have general liability insurance, do you also need to have the company and employees bonded? The answer is — sometimes, yes. Liability insurance covers accidental property damage or injury caused by you, the contractor, to your customer's property or people on the site, but it does not compensate for construction defects or poor workmanship. A surety bond is an agreement that the contractor arranges with a bonding company to pay awards to the consumer if the contractor is judged at fault by arbitration or legal action if a job is not completed to the customer's satisfaction. For example, in a painting business, a customer can claim that the paint job was sloppy, not up to the quality expected, or not completed on time. State laws differ, but it is common for states to require contractors to carry surety bonds of a certain level, depending on their license category. Bonding is usually a requirement for jobs with the government or large commercial jobs. If you are a small-scale painting business that takes on large commercial jobs, then you will want to be bonded. Surety bonds, also called performance bonds, are available from insurance companies. If you cannot get such coverage on the commercial market, the SBA has a surety bond program that might be available to you — but, as with all government programs, be prepared for paperwork.

Although it is expensive to carry both liability insurance and a surety bond, it helps attract and keep customers who understand that their property and investment will be protected — no matter what. Plus, you can then charge premium rates, because not every person in the painting business carries this coverage. You can find a bond provider who works with businesses in your state at the National Association of Surety Bond Producers' website (**www.nasbp.org**). When you visit the site, click on "Need a Bond" and then choose "Find a Producer in Your State." When you click on your state on the map, a list of providers and their contact information will be listed for you.

Employee bonding is a different matter. Employee dishonesty bonds are surety bonds that guarantee compensation if your employee steals property or is otherwise negligent on the job. You might want this coverage because, frankly, you never know what another person is thinking. Talk to your insurance agent to see if it is necessary.

Home-based business insurance

Home-based insurance will be required if you are working out of an office in your home, which you might be doing when you first start your faux painting or mural design business. Homeowners' policies rarely cover business losses. If you are operating from your home or garage, check with your insurance agent to see whether anything in your office is covered. The typical homeowner's policy specifically excludes home-based business losses, including equipment, theft, loss of data, and personal injury. Unfortunately, many companies that provide homeowner's insurance do not offer business coverage, so you might need to have two insurance companies covering different areas of your home.

Criminal insurance

Criminal insurance covers you in the event that an employee commits a crime during work hours. General liability insurance might not cover theft or other criminal acts by employees. If someone is on your payroll, you can be held responsible for his or her actions while he or she is with customers. Should that person steal, vandalize customer property, or deliberately harm someone, the customer will expect you to assume responsibility. This type of coverage can also protect you in the event of employee embezzlement. Depending on your general liability coverage, you might want to consider this category of insurance when you decide to hire employees.

Key man insurance

Lenders who provide capital for businesses might require key man insurance. This coverage applies to the person whose absence from the company would cause it to fail. Most likely, that person would be you or your partner. If you have borrowed money to start or operate your business, the lender might require such insurance as a guarantee of payment if anything were to happen to you.

Business interruption insurance

Business interruption insurance covers your expenses if you are shut down by fire, natural disaster, or other catastrophes. Some businesses are not as vulnerable to this as other types of businesses, so look carefully at your other coverage. Assuming your equipment and vehicles are already covered, you might not want to duplicate coverage. Discuss this with your provider or broker.

Vehicle insurance

Vehicle insurance is the commercial version of the insurance you have on your private vehicle. The same price considerations apply: type of vehicle, history of claims, mileage, location, and drivers. If you have employees who will drive your vehicles, their driving records will be considered in the rate you pay, along with yours.

4

Rendering Your Office and Staff

"Nothing is really work unless you would rather be doing something else."

~ James M. Barrie (1860–1937), *Author of Peter Pan*

As your painting business begins to take shape, you will need adequate space to keep track of all the things that come in and go out to keep your enterprise moving forward and growing. It might be a desk, an unused guest room, or on occasion, a rented space. Most painters begin their office at home and many stay there. As a service business, you do not need a space for products to be displayed and sold. This is one advantage that a service business has over a retail business because it cuts your overhead considerably. More than half of America's small businesses are home-based, according to the SBA, and a home office might be ideal in the beginning because you will be starting small. You will need to have or create space for it, and hopefully, your community allows home-based businesses.

Let's examine the zoning issue first. Many communities have restrictions on businesses based in private homes, mostly because of the traffic and other issues associated with operating a business. Although heavy traffic should not be an issue for a painting business, check your local zoning. You can do a Web search for your local government or look up the number in the phonebook. Explain what you plan to do. Tell them that you do not expect your business to cause an increase in traffic because you will be going to the customers rather than having them come to you. You might be required to pay a license fee.

Assuming it is legal for you to base your business at home, why would you want to? For starters, the commute is great. You do not have to pay rent, and there can be some tax benefits, too. The IRS has strict guidelines for claiming a home office as a business expense, so discuss the details with your accountant. Plus, as a painter, you will want to spend the majority of your work time in the field. Your office will be the place where you fill in the essential details of making calls, bookkeeping, and of course, sketching and designing plans for clients.

Can You Succeed Working Out of Your Home?

Not everyone can afford a studio away from home — and not everyone needs one. Interior painters might not need a studio, but for a decorative painter, having a space in your home to paint, sketch, design plans, and experiment with paint is essential. It could be a corner of a room in your home or, if you are lucky, a whole room that you can convert into a studio. If you are going to operate as a sole proprietorship or a partnership, then a small space is feasible, but as your business grows, so will your need for space. It is often quite possible to succeed with a home-based painting business. You should consider what you need and how you can make that work. These considerations should include:

- **Can you create the space you need?** Most people find they can repurpose a guest room or remodel a garage to build their office or studio.

- **How much will you be on location?** If you work mostly outside your home, you might get away with a computer on the dining room table and an easel or table for painting.

- **Do you have room?** Where can you find the space? Look at your home environment to determine whether you have space for an easel, a drawing board, and a desk where you can keep up with all aspects of managing your business. Ideally, you will be able to set aside a small section of your home dedicated to all things painting and business.

- **Will there be a good working environment?** If you have small children at home, and you absolutely cannot afford an outside office, you will have to work at home with your small children. But, if the home environment makes work difficult and you can afford outside space, it is probably worth the cost to rent an outside office or studio.

- **Are you disciplined enough to work from home?** This is one of the first questions many people have when they consider working out of their homes. The fact is, some people simply cannot get past the distractions of having their family around or the temptations of television or visiting friends. For them, having an office outside the house to get their work done is ideal.

Collective Workspaces

Are you the type that needs somewhere to go every day in order to be more productive? You might want to consider using mobile technology, such as a cell phone and laptop computer, to take your office with you. This could be a good option for painters who spend much time away from the office. With this method, you can do the majority of your work on the road and some of the other tasks, such as sketching and filing papers, from your home. Also, if you do not want to pay for a studio or rent an office, you can look into using incubators or collective workspace environments.

Since the technology boom in the 1990s, the concept of small business incubator programs has grown from offering support to only technology-oriented companies to offering support to businesses of all types. The National Business Incubation Association website (**www. nbia.org**) defines business incubation as a business support process that accelerates the successful development of start-up and fledgling companies by providing entrepreneurs with an array of targeted resources and services. Among these services is often the access to shared or sole office space.

Incubation services tend to be managed through an organizational management arm and offer a network of contacts, both within and outside the incubation organization. Accessibility to offices and meeting rooms is just one of the benefits of participating in an incubator program. Another benefit is the opportunity to network with other people in your industry who are also in a similar start-up phase and have similar needs.

You might also want to consider forming a collective with other people in creative industries for the purpose of networking or sharing office space. For instance, if you are a faux painter, consider sharing space with an interior painter or designer. It might be beneficial. Not only would you be able to share resources and split costs, but you would also be able to share leads, brainstorm, and work on joint marketing efforts.

Setting Up Your Office

If you are planning to operate your business from home, you will need cooperation. Explain to your family that you are going to need to reserve a room; then, plan your workspace. Make sure it is large enough to be comfortable and efficient for everything you will do there, including painting and sketching, as well as the day-to-day aspects of marketing, scheduling, payroll, and more. You will need space for a large desk, file cabinets, a computer, a printer, a drafting table or easel, and at least two chairs. You may want to set up an extra place for an assistant to answer the phones or do bookkeeping when you are out. You will need at least a small bookcase. Look to the future. Will you still have room to run your business in that space in a year?

Choose a quiet spot. You cannot work well if there are kids yelling, trains going by, dogs barking, and a television in the background. If a client needs to visit your office, you will not present a professional appearance if a customer has to ask, "What's that noise?" You will not be giving your business the attention and focus it needs if you are distracted.

Phone

While you can start a business with no more than the above essentials, you will probably do better with a few extras. If you want to be listed in the yellow pages, you will need to have a phone line dedicated to business. Some people only use a cell phone, but the dedicated line is preferable. It is more expensive, but you can also receive faxes this way. Use the landline telephone as your official business telephone number and forward calls to your cell phone or an answering machine or service. You also might want a fax machine if you would like a faster way to send and receive signed contracts and other paperwork and possibly a dedicated fax line, which can double as a second business line for calls if necessary. If you choose to use your cell phone as your primary business number, you may regret it when your phone rings constantly at job sites. An answering machine on an office line can be accessed remotely, so you will always be able to check your messages, even from job sites.

A two-line business phone is not a luxury. Line one is typically designated as the primary business line. Line two can be assigned as the fax line and also used to make outgoing calls. Some phone companies offer a "distinctive ring" feature that rings differently if a fax is coming in, so you do not make a mistake and pick up the phone. Telephone prices vary according to quality and features. Find the best one you can afford. Consider models with caller ID and automatic dialing. If you do not plan to use an answering service, consider a telephone with a built-in answering device. Callers will leave messages for you and the device will tell you when they called, so you can prioritize your call returns. You can save yourself some neck discomfort with frequent calls by getting a headset.

Appointment calendar

An appointment calendar can be as simple as any wall calendar — just make sure it is accessible and easy to see. Do not let your appointments get randomly scribbled into notebooks or scattered on scraps of paper. Loose pieces of paper that are stuffed into pockets or notebooks are hard to keep track of and keeping all appointments is essential for any business owner. When you miss appointments with clients or vendors, you not only miss out on work, but can quickly create a bad name for yourself. Aside from the standard wall calendar, keep a portable appointment book that goes everywhere with you. It will prevent you from writing down an appointment date or a new client's phone number on an old receipt from the floor of your car when away from home.

Fax machine, copier, and scanner

Unless you plan to use your local copy store for faxes, you will need a fax machine. All-in-one machines are used by many small businesses for faxing, copying, and scanning. The prices are reasonable, and they work well. Models that are more expensive have extra features and might be more durable. These are inkjet printers, not laser machines, which cost significantly more money.

Calculator

You will need at least two. Your office should have a desktop calculator. They are easier to use, have larger number pads, provide printouts of your calculations, and have features needed for working up bids, such as mark up/mark down. Attach the printouts to your office copy of bids as a way to check your base numbers later in the bidding process.

If you add a zero or two in your calculations, it is nice to know where the problem occurred. The second calculator can be a small pocket model, cell phone, or PDA that you will use in the field for quick bids, balances, and other calculating needs.

Office supplies

Standard office supplies include letterheads, envelopes, business cards, and printer ink cartridges. Let's consider the letterhead first. You want a professional look that features your company's name, telephone number, fax number, and your address. If you are working out of your home and do not feel comfortable revealing this to customers, you may prefer to use a post office box for your business mail. You will want a return address where people can safely send payments. If you want a logo or something beyond basic type, you may wish to have a graphic designer create something simple, professional, and easy to read. You can also choose a tasteful sample from a quick-printer's sample book. There are templates in most word processing programs that can be adapted for your needs as well. This method allows you to print a basic letterhead on your own computer.

Envelopes should reflect your letterhead in style and tone. Use business-sized envelopes (Number 10s). If you decide to include a return envelope, it should be a Number 9, to fit inside with your statement.

A Number 10 envelope will accept standard letterhead, folded horizontally in thirds. There are two types: window and closed envelopes. Window envelopes are frequently used by businesses because the mailing address of the intended party on the inside form shows through the envelope's window. Closed envelopes require that the address of the recipient be separately posted, either by printing it on the envelope or using a pre-printed sticker. If you decide not to have envelopes printed and do not want to run them through your computer printer, you can either print labels with your return address or purchase a rubber stamp. When you buy rubber stamps, consider getting one imprinted with "For Deposit Only" and your bank account number to protect checks from being forged if they are inadvertently lost or stolen before you take them to the bank.

Business cards are essential. You will pass them around to virtually everyone you meet; potential customers are everywhere. You never know when a customer will walk into your life. Business cards should be easy to read. There is nothing more irritating than staring at a business card that has so much information you cannot find the number to call or the service being offered. The card should state your company's name, your name and title, a primary phone number, fax number, e-mail address, and possibly your cell number. As you can see, the card is already busy with just the basics. A simple logo, or none at all, is fine. Get the cards professionally printed to give them a professional appearance. You can go to one of the office supply or chain printers for cards, letterhead, and other such items at a reasonable cost. You also might find companies on the Internet that will offer quick turnaround at low prices for such products. You may also want pre-printed invoices, estimate sheets, and service lists. It is acceptable to print these yourself on your computer as long as they look professional.

Transportation

It is important to note that your vehicle will be your portable office and should be treated as such. As a professional painter, you will be dependent on your car, truck, or van to get you and all your supplies to the work site. Your vehicle should be in good working order, insured, and able to haul all your supplies, such as buckets, paint, and ladders. Make sure to keep some basic office supplies in your car, such as spare business cards, sketchpads, a calculator, and an appointment calendar.

Computers and Software

Personal computers (PCs) based on IBM's® original model and Apple® Macintosh computers (Macs) and their variants are both fine for your business. Macs may be less virus-prone, although that is changing. They are considered very reliable, but also more expensive and have fewer specialty business software programs designed to work with them because there are fewer Macs in most businesses. There is an ongoing debate as to whether Macs are better for artists. PCs have been given a stuffy business-only stereotype. There are fans on both sides. There is design software for each, and specifically interior design software, which will allow you to give your client a virtual look at their repainted space. 3D Home Inventor Deluxe is one program for PCs. The same program for Macs is called Live Interior 3D, but it is a little more expensive.

PCs are often less expensive and have thousands of software programs available, so you can do more shopping around. The price of PCs has come down so much it would be hard to justify purchasing a used one. Some new PCs are in the $500 range, including a monitor. Do not forget that whatever you buy will probably be out of date in a couple of years.

Your first consideration is what you need to operate your business. You are going to access the Internet, probably with a cable, wireless, or DSL broadband connection, so you will need speed and power for that.

As a professional decorative painter or muralist, you will be downloading and processing photo files regularly, so you need a large hard drive, at least 320 GB, to store the photos. You will need Adobe® PhotoShop® or other photo processing software and probably a scanner, as well as a color printer, either inkjet or laser.

Most likely, you will be keeping your books on the computer, processing orders, maintaining files, creating spreadsheets, faxing, storing, and printing. Use software programs that help with tasks specifically related to your business.

Explain your needs to the computer companies or retailers you are dealing with and compare their responses. If you have friends or family members who are more computer savvy than you are, ask them for their advice.

Desktop or laptop?

Both options have benefits and drawbacks. The desktop computer will probably have a bigger screen and an easy-to-use-keyboard. A desktop might cost less than a laptop, but you cannot take it into the field to use for presentations and proposals. A laptop is portable and easy to use, but it costs more. The cheapest route is to select the most powerful desktop you can afford to get the most computing power for your money. You can purchase a laptop when your business has grown and you have more cash to spend.

You might want to purchase an external hard drive to back up, or archive, your document files and other essential records at least once a week to avoid data catastrophes. Back up, or copy and archive, all-important data including designs, invoices, and your financial records at least daily or every time you work on a file.

You might also want to consider an online-backup system, in addition to backing up your computer locally to an external hard drive. An external hard drive is a place outside your main tower that plugs in with an interface cable. It is a great place to store large quantities of music photos, or other media files, which will free up space on your internal drive. It is also a good idea to save private documents such as those that contain financial information on your external hard drive. Many threats to the information on your internal hard drive exist including spyware and viruses. By keeping important files on your external drive, they are safe as long as you turn it off or unplug it from your computer when you use the Internet. The external hard drive is also handy in that it is portable to other computers.

There are also two reasonably priced online backup options offered by Mozy (**www.mozy.com**) and Ibackup (**www.ibackup.com**). These sites allow you to backup your files online as opposed to purchasing an external hard drive. Regular backups protect your data from electrical blackouts, viruses, and other calamities.

Business software

Your new computer will come with the software necessary to operate, whether it is a PC or Mac. It will probably come with a word processing program, Internet browser, an e-mail program, and other programs that the manufacturer includes with the initial purchase.

PCs often come with Microsoft® Office, an office suite that includes Word, Excel®, PowerPoint®, and Internet Explorer®. You can purchase similar software for a Mac (the Pages software), but Macs also work well with Microsoft products. There are many other word processing programs, some of them free (check the OpenOffice website at **www.openoffice.org** for samples). Realistically, at this time, it is a Microsoft world in business, and if you want to easily transfer files to other companies for bids and proposals, you can assume they want them in Word. Beware of word-processing or other programs whose functionality is limited.

Secure an Accountant or Purchase Accounting Software

Deciding whether to secure an accountant or purchase financial software for your business's accounting needs will ultimately be up to you. It all depends on the size of your operation as well as your knowledge of accounting principles. If you feel comfortable enough to keep your accounting records, then purchasing good accounting software should suffice. However, it is recommended that you still have an accountant look over the business records at the end of the year to ensure accuracy when it comes to closing out the year and filing tax returns. There are several accounting software packages available in the market today, but you have to be careful which one you choose. Some are very limited and only include payroll, invoicing, and general recordkeeping. One of the most widely used packages, known for its all-encompassing versatility, is QuickBooks™ financial software. The basic version of this program, QuickBooks Pro, sells for approximately $199.95 at office supply retailers and has the capability of invoicing; keeping track of sales tax, income, and expenses; and printing checks. QuickBooks'

"Premier Edition" is a complete accounting system for your business and more. You can create forecasts, a business plan, and even do your budgeting, and it sells for approximately $399.95. QuickBooks can also be purchased online directly from the QuickBooks website at **http://quickbooks.intuit.com** or other sites such as Amazon.com.

If your strengths are not in accounting and recordkeeping, you should secure the services of an accountant, at least during the first year of operations or until you are comfortable enough to do the company's recordkeeping yourself. Accurate recordkeeping is essential in maintaining your finances, and sometimes this is something that only an accountant can do accurately. Knowing exactly where you stand financially at any given time will influence a number of business decisions that must be made on short notice and will either help or hinder your company financially.

Accounting software

There are numerous brands of accounting software. Some are so popular that other software providers create "add-ons" that improve the functionality of the software. Again, there are many choices and you should work with your accountant to coordinate bookkeeping with her or him.

QuickBooks is one of the most widely used programs. It is offered in both PC and Mac versions. There are small-business versions that allow you to balance your checkbook, do your payroll, track expenses by category, and create custom forms. You will want to discuss all of the accounting details of your business with your accountant before you set up your books so you are on the same page. QuickBooks takes a little practice to use effectively, but it is not difficult if you take an hour or two to get the basics, set up accounts, and gain some understanding of what it does. QuickBooks offers a contractor edition that allows you to track job costs and profits and to manage progress on several jobs at once.

However, QuickBooks is not the only highly rated business accounting program available. Peachtree, MYOB Business Essentials™, NetSuite® Small Business Accounting, and Simply Accounting Pro are others. They all provide the basic features you need to run your business and offer special features besides helping to balance your checkbook and calculate payroll taxes. They offer sophisticated business applications that can help you keep track of how much you are spending on paint and other supplies and compare your costs to how much money you are generating from painting jobs.

Once you have a good accounting program and set up categories, such as expenditures and income, set up correctly, you will not need your accountant every day. Instead, your accountant can do weekly, monthly, or even quarterly oversight and monitoring. If you do not enjoy working with the figures, you can choose to hire a part-time bookkeeper to maintain the numbers and perform data entry. However, if you hire someone else to oversee your financial resources, check the records periodically to be sure everything adds up, or ask your accountant to review your employee's work if you do not understand it. Companies of every size have had to grapple with misuse of funds or embezzlement. The best way to prevent this is to monitor the books or have someone you trust do it for you.

Obviously, you will want to start your business financial dealings by using a separate business bank account. It is confusing and risky to comingle your personal funds with the business resources. Maintain a business checking account under the business name. Deposit all business checks into that account. Have credit card payments deposited there. If a customer pays you cash, deposit the money into the business account. If you are operating as a sole proprietorship, and need to pay yourself for the work you have performed, write a check from the business account to yourself and then deposit it into your personal account. Run your business squeaky clean to avoid nasty problems tomorrow. The following are some basic accounting terms you may want to discuss with your accountant; together you can decide what will work best for your particular situation:

- **Cash versus accrual:** The cash method is recording a sale when the money is received and an expense recorded when the cash goes out. This measures only what happens in your business, not necessarily when you made the sale. Accrual is recording the income when you invoice the job and recording expenses when they are incurred, not when they are paid.

- **Double entry versus single entry:** Double means every one of your business entries is registered twice: once as a debit and once as a credit. You must be sure that everything balances — dollars are recorded coming in and going out. Single-entry bookkeeping is easier but is more prone to mistakes because there is no automatic balance. Your accountant will probably use the double-entry system.

- **Debit versus credit:** Debit is the payout. Credit is where you got the money. Your company buys a rake. The rake is a debit. The money to pay for the rake is the credit.

- **Calendar year versus fiscal year:** Businesses operate on a 12-month cycle. Theoretically, it can begin at any time of year. If your business operates on a calendar year, your annual bookkeeping will begin on January 1 and end on December 31. If you operate your business on a fiscal year, it means you begin your 12-month bookkeeping cycle some time after January 1 and end it 12 months after that. For instance, the federal government's fiscal year begins October 1. Some business structures, such as sole proprietorships, are required to operate on a calendar year. Whichever way you maintain your books, your business-year structure is important for tax issues and to anchor your annual business planning and assessment.

It is critically important to keep accurate and detailed books. There are many terms and systems, but nothing is as important as committing yourself to fine bookkeeping. You must keep track of all accounts, income, and expenses. This is critical to the health and growth of your company. It is the only way you can know how your business is doing and whether you are meeting projections. It is the method by which you will track the effectiveness of your marketing because your record keeping will tell you where your leads come from, what your closing rate is, how much your average customer spends, what services they need (and request), what your materials cost, how much you pay your employees, and all of the other small and large details of operating a successful business. Use the best software that offers the most small business support.

Business planning software can assist you in putting your business plan together, as well as plan its growth and future. Palo Alto Software offers software called Business Plan Pro®, which provides hundreds of sample business plans as examples and helps you work through the process of putting your own plan together. Business Plan Writer Deluxe and Ultimate Business Planner® are two other options for planning software. HomeOfficeReports.com reviews business-planning software and evaluates based on things like ease of use, cost, support, features, and compatible software. The cost of this type of software is $50 to $1,000, depending on features, sophistication, and other factors. You probably do not need business-planning software that can support a Fortune 500 company. A program that can help you put your business together and plan for growth is adequate. Beware of loading your computer with too many large programs that slow down your operating system. Look over your business planning software options and pick one that meets your needs. Remember, if you are using QuickBooks Pro or another high-quality accounting program, it will contain some of the planning elements you need, so you do not need to duplicate these features with another program. For a small, start-up business, it is a good idea to keep things simple.

A few more software recommendations for painters are:

- **Goldenseal:** Software specifically designed for painting contractors that helps you run the business side.

- **ServiceCEO:** Ideal for painters, as it helps track customers, jobs, and schedules.

- **Color Style Studio 2.4:** Wins over your customers by taking photos of their space and shows them how it will look after painting with various colors. The color choices are from the top paint manufacturers.

Computer security

Firewalls and virus protection programs are essential tools in computer protection. European Union computer security experts estimated in 2007 that viruses begin to attack new computers on the Internet within seconds. Firewalls — whether hardware, software, or a combination of the two — protect your computer from unwelcome intrusions.

Virus protection programs protect your computer against specific, known viruses. Symantec™, McAfee®, and Norton™ are among the best-known software providers of this type of protection. Their programs must be updated regularly — preferably every day — to guard against the latest viruses, so you will want a renewable subscription, less than $100 annually for the basics.

If you are already familiar with computers, you are probably conscious of spammers, who send out millions of e-mail messages for products or services you have never requested, and the "phishing" schemes they pursue. If not, you need to know that dishonest computer hackers constantly try to steal your passwords, bank account numbers, and other personal or business identity information to steal your money or your identity. The simplest way to protect yourself is to never click a link sent by someone you do not know, especially if the person claims to be a "webmaster" at a bank, your Internet service provider, or some other legitimate-sounding source. If you are doubtful, phone the company that is supposedly requesting the information from you. You must make sure you have every resource available to help protect your computer against the latest schemes of hackers who want to access your bank accounts, credit cards, passwords, and all of the other information you need to protect.

Hiring Employees

In the beginning, your painting business will be a company of one, unless you have a partner. In the future, however, you might need to hire some help. You might encounter a mural large enough to warrant an extra pair of hands. Or, as an interior painter, you might begin to have more than one job at a time or land a job painting an entire apartment complex. If so, as a muralist, a great place to find help is with your local artist association. It can put you in touch with people who have the skills and painting experience you will need to match your own. Placing an ad, either in the newspaper or on Craigslist, is also an option. Be sure whoever responds can present you with a portfolio, so you can see whether his or her painting skills are a match for you. If you are hiring an extra interior painter, be sure he or she can provide you with a résumé and references. Being able to get in touch with an applicant's professional references will give you a sense of whether he or she is reliable and trustworthy.

After your business is underway and you start going out to quote jobs or work in the field, you might decide that a phone answering machine is not enough. There are definite advantages in having someone in the office to answer the phones, call the vendors, and do phone marketing or set schedules for bidding. Some of this work cannot wait until dark when the outside jobs are completed.

You might want to tiptoe into the role of employing an office worker. Part-time help is usually easy to come by. You might simply ask around among friends or relatives. If you are reluctant to take a chance on a friend's recommendation, and you live in an urban or suburban area, place a classified ad in your local paper or online publication or on a local/national site such as Craigslist (**www.craigslist.org**) or Monster (**www.monster.com**). You will probably receive more job applications than you can handle.

Start the selection process before you place the ad by describing exactly what you want your new employee to do, what experience he or she will need before starting, and what software programs or equipment skills the person will need to have previous experience in. Also, remember that your helper might well become the "face and voice" of your business. The person you choose should be able to get along with the public — in person and on the phone. You might want someone who can also do cold calling to solicit business for an extra bonus if an appointment is actually set. Or, perhaps you would rather have a bookkeeper to take over some of the data entry responsibilities. Whatever it is you want, write it down, read it over several times, and picture the type of person you would feel comfortable with. Personality counts.

Discriminatory Practices

Under Title VII, the ADA, and the ADEA, it is illegal to discriminate in any aspect of employment, including:

- Hiring and firing
- Compensation, assignment, or classification of employees

- Transfer, promotion, layoff, or recall

- Job advertisements

- Recruitment

- Testing

- Use of company facilities

- Training and apprenticeship programs

- Fringe benefits

- Pay, retirement plans, and disability leave

- Other terms and conditions of employment

Discriminatory practices under these laws also include:

- Harassment based on race, color, religion, sex, national origin, disability, or age.

- Retaliation against an individual for filing a charge of discrimination, participating in an investigation, or opposing discriminatory practices.

- Employment decisions based on stereotypes or assumptions about the abilities, traits, or performance of individuals of a certain sex, race, age, religion, or ethnic group, or individuals with disabilities.

- Denying employment opportunities to a person because of marriage to, or association with, an individual of a particular race, religion, national origin, or an individual with a disability. Title VII also prohibits discrimination because of participation in schools or places of worship associated with a particular racial, ethnic, or religious group.

Be an effective employer and leader

Employers are required to post notices to all employees advising them of their rights under the laws that EEOC enforces and their right to be free from retaliation. Such notices must be accessible to persons with visual or other disabilities that affect reading.

These guidelines should be followed by all business people, even small, start-up businesses like yours. Once you select a person to hire, you will need to set up a personnel file for him or her, prepare the appropriate government paperwork for tax withholding, and other new-hire policies. If you are not sure what is required, your accountant, state tax officer, or local chamber of commerce can point you in the right direction.

You will also want to set aside some concentrated time to train your new employee in the way you want the business to be handled. He or she might be spending a lot of "alone time" in the office or in the field. Make sure your painter knows and follows your codes of conduct at the work site in regard to setup and cleanup procedures. Let him or her know whether it is acceptable to play music while working, which may disrupt the environment of a home or office. Make sure he or she knows that the work site is not a place for friends or family to visit unless it is cleared by you first. You will want to closely monitor the results of the work you assign to be sure the job is done. With any luck, there will be no problems, but if there are, you will have to retrain or fire the individual. Neither of these tasks is much fun; it is much easier to pick your employee carefully from the start.

Finally, because you hired an office worker to take the burden off yourself, you will want to see some payback in terms of increased revenue within a fairly short period of time. Be sure you do a cost analysis of your hiring experiment to see if it is bringing you more income or costing you more money than you expected. When hiring office help for your painting business, make sure the person is experienced and has a good performance record in the areas of scheduling and customer relations in order to represent your business well.

Ideally, you will find someone who has knowledge and experience in painting. If you come across this type of individual, find out why he or she is not employed. Experience alone is not a good indicator of a satisfactory employee. After all, this person might have been fired because he or she was not dependable or competent. Successful business managers recommend zero tolerance for any bad behavior, whether it is showing up late, laziness, or constant complaining without getting anything done. Make your policies clear from day one and put them in writing, so there will be no misunderstandings if you fire someone at the job site.

So where do you find employees for your business? It is not unusual for prospective employees to contact businesses looking for work. They might see your truck or notice you at a job site and offer their services. Eager, experienced workers might drop into your lap, especially when the economy is not doing well. When times are good, you might have to be a little more proactive in your search.

Newspaper or Internet ads are effective. Put one together outlining exactly what you are looking for, including the work and hours, but consider whether you want to put the hourly pay in the ad. In some areas of the country, help-wanted ads routinely contain the starting hourly wage. In others, a wage range is listed, and in other places, words such as "competitive hourly wage" are used instead of specific numbers. Get to know the pay scales in your area for the work you want done and check the ads being placed by your competitors and use those standards as guides. Also, be sure to state in your ad that applicants must be currently eligible to work in the United State for any employer.

This is the only "prescreening" you can legally do to make sure you are not hiring an ineligible worker. If you live in a large metropolitan area, you might get better results from community papers than from the large dailies that cover areas of 100 or more miles. Online services, such as Craigslist and its local competitors, might be a cost effective form of advertising. Just be sure your applicants are local. It is not wise to employ someone who lives two hours away and drives an old car that might or might not start on any given day.

Keep in mind that it is illegal to place an ad that discriminates against anyone because of race, sex, age, religion, and other factors. You are looking for someone who can do the job, no matter what other qualities the person has or does not have. List your telephone number and/or e-mail address in the ad rather than an address or post office box number. If you list your address and you are working out of your home, you might have unexpected visitors at your door at all hours. Using a post office box will delay response time, so is not desirable for hiring in a rush.

Interviews

The interview process begins on the telephone, as you are setting a time for a personal meeting. The first thing to consider is the attitude of the person on the other end. Is he or she friendly or surly? Do not confuse an inability to articulate with a bad attitude. Someone might not have much formal education, but he or she might have experience and a positive attitude that will overcome poor grammar. What is the overall demeanor of the person you are talking to on the telephone? Does this sound like a person you would like to be around? Some people might be shy about admitting they do not have much experience or some other negative issue. Lack of experience is not as big a drawback as someone whom you suspect is being evasive and trying to pass off work experience at a fast food restaurant as a qualification to work for you as an employee.

Why do they want the job? Do they have an interest in painting, or do they just need some money? Select the most suitable applicants before you schedule face-to-face meetings. You will want to know whether they have experience with the tools and equipment they will be using as your employee.

During the personal interview, apply the same standards you would expect your customers to use. How is this person presenting himself or herself? Is the person clean? Is clothing torn or dirty? Does he or she look you in the eye? If the prospective employee claims to have experience, ask him or her two or three questions that require some knowledge to answer. You do not have to be challenging or harsh in your questioning. You can be friendly, even funny. You simply want to determine to the best of your ability whether this person is being honest with you. You might want to present a scenario and ask how the applicant would start, perform, and finish the task you describe.

Review the applicant's résumé and ask questions about gaps in work history, lack of recommendations, or past employers. Someone who tries to turn that work history into a major qualification to work for you might not be as desirable as an employee. If you have the sense that your candidate is lying, be cautious about hiring him or her. It is easier to not hire someone in the first place than to fire him or her after the fact.

Before you interview anyone, read the rules about discrimination in hiring. Some questions are forbidden. You cannot ask about a person's religion, politics, or sexual preference. Your questions should track the qualifications for the job, not outside interests or qualities the prospect has no control over. That same standard would not apply to an office worker whose most challenging physical effort will be moving paper from one side of a desk to another or using the telephone.

It is not out of bounds to ask "what if" questions during a job interview. "What if there is heavy lifting involved or you have to stay late to finish a job on time?" is an appropriate question. Test his or her knowledge on painting procedures by asking what the applicant would do if he or she spills paint on a customer's floor. Ask the applicant what he or she would do to prevent such an accident. Discuss the job with the applicant, describing in detail what you would want that person to do. Check the person's reactions. If the candidate responds in a way that is completely unreasonable, smile, thank him for his time, and end the interview. Also, avoid the applicant whose interview style is to present a list of demands he or she expects you to meet.

With each job applicant, try to view the person objectively. Is this someone you want to be around every day? Someone a customer would like and trust? Someone you believe can help your company grow? All of these things matter.

Hiring people you can promote is important because it gives employees reassurance they can grow along with your company and provides incentives for superior performance. Ambition can work for you. Do not be reluctant to hire the smartest people you can find.

Once you have narrowed your list and found the person or persons you would like to hire, check them out. Call former employers to inquire about their work histories and performance. Be aware that many former employers will be reluctant to offer bad news about someone. Know the qualities you want to inquire about and ask specific questions. If you just ask, "What can you tell me about Bob?" you will probably get an answer as general as the question. "He was all right." You want to know if Bob showed up on time, did what he was supposed to do, and caused any problems. Ask whether Bob was tidy on the work site and whether his painting work was professional or sloppy. Listen for what Bob's former employer is not telling you. If his former employer is distant or does not seem as though he or she has much to say about Bob, this might be a warning sign. On the other hand, if he or she says, "I would hire him again in a minute," you have the answer you need.

Once you have made a decision, call Bob and give him the good news. Tell him clearly, as you should have done during the interview, that you have a probationary period of 60 or 90 days — longer or shorter as you choose — during which he can quit or you can let him go with no hard feelings and no obligation on either side. Send him a confirmation letter outlining your work policies and what is expected of him in the areas of punctuality at the work site, appropriate dress, and safety regulations with materials and personal property. This can be a separate document if you like. Again, as with customers, it is best to have all requirements and expectations in writing.

Contact everyone else you have interviewed and explain that you have made a decision to hire someone else, and keep the résumés of people you think might be suitable in the future. Wish everyone well and thank them for their time.

Some communities restrict how many employees a home-based business can have. Check your local zoning and other regulations before you commit to a number of people parking their cars and doing other business-related activities in the neighborhood. If you face such restrictions, you will be forced to either rent business space or arrange to meet all of your workers at job sites or other locations.

New employee paperwork

No matter whom you hire, you will have to fill out and send in or retain certain government documents. These include W-4 forms, the Employee's Withholding Allowance Certificate, and the W-5, for employees with a child, if they qualify for advance payment of earned income credit. Check the IRS site (**www.irs.gov**) or Business.gov (**http://business.gov/business-law/forms**) to download forms. You can also find various employee paperwork on the CD-ROM included with this book.

Application of Federal Law to Employers

A number of factors can cause an employer to be covered by a federal employment law. These include the number of employees employed by a business — whether an employer is a private entity or a branch of federal, state, or local government — and the type of industry an employer is in.

The following chart shows how the number of workers a company employs determines whether a specific federal statute applies to the business:

NUMBER OF EMPLOYEES	APPLICABLE STATUTE
100	WARN — Worker Adjustment and Retraining Notification Act
50	FMLA — Family Medical Leave Act
20	ADEA — Age Discrimination in Employment Act
20	COBRA — Consolidated Omnibus Benefits Reconciliation Act
20	OWBPA — Older Workers Benefit Protection Act
15	ADA — American with Disabilities Act
15	GINA — Genetic Information Nondiscrimination Act
15	Title VII of the Civil Rights Act of 1964
15	PDA — Pregnancy Discrimination Act
1	EPPA — Employee Polygraph Protection Act
1	EPA — Equal Pay Act
1	FRCA — Fair Credit Reporting Act
1	FLSA — Fair Labor Standards Act

1	IRCA — Immigration Reform and Control Act
1	OSHA — Occupational Safety and Health Act
1	PRWORA — Personal Responsibility and Work Opportunity Reconciliation Act
1	USERRA — Uniform Services Employment and Reemployment Rights Act

Creating an Ethical Environment

Creating an ethical culture in the workplace is a process that takes time, investment, and continual education. For an ethical culture to become established, both management and employees must be committed to it and willing to live by it every day. When employees feel that they are safe and treated fairly, they will be happier and better workers. Creating an ethical environment can also keep you out of trouble with lawsuits in the areas of discrimination and sexual harassment.

Ethics policy or code of conduct

Every organization should have a formal ethics policy because it legally supports efforts to enforce ethical conduct in the workplace. Employees who have read and signed a formal ethics policy cannot claim they were unaware their conduct was unacceptable. Recommended codes of conduct for various types of organizations are commercially available, but every organization should tailor its own ethics policy to suit its business and its needs. A good ethics policy is simple and easy to understand, addresses general conduct, and offers a few examples to explain how the code might be applied. It should not contain myriad rules to cover specific situations or threats such as "violators will be prosecuted to the full extent of the law." In a legal trial of a fraud perpetrator, it is the judge and not the company that will decide the sentence. An ethics policy or code of conduct should cover:

- **General conduct at work.** Explain that ethical and honest behavior is expected of all employees and they are expected to act in the best interests of the company.

- **Conflicts of interest.** Employees might not understand what does and does not constitute a conflict of interest, so some simple examples are appropriate. For example, you would not want employees to have a second job with a competing company.

- **Confidentiality.** This involves a company's policy on the sharing of information among employees and departments or with people outside the company. If your employees are privy to your company's financial state, explain that it is not to be discussed with anyone else.

- **Relationships with vendors and customers.** This involves a company's policy regarding doing business with a relative, friend, or personal acquaintance. Clarify whether a discount would be offered on a paint job to the employee's friends or family.

- **Gifts.** You should declare your policy regarding the types and amounts of gifts that can be accepted or given by employees during the course of doing business. Sometimes, clients will give tips to people who provide services to their home or office. Discuss whether this is acceptable or not.

- **Relationships with the media**. You should describe your company's policy regarding who should communicate with the media about company affairs. Your employees might be approached by advertisers or even reporters. If you want to handle all matters relating to media coverage, then say so. If you are comfortable with your employees handling these matters, then state that.

- **Use of the organization's assets for personal purposes.** This section should cover personal use of the Internet while at work and use of copy machines, telephones, and company vehicles.

- **Procedure for reporting unethical behavior.** Employees should be encouraged to report any ethical violation, large or small. This section should explain how and to whom reports should be submitted and the use of a tip hotline if one exists.

- **Consequences of unethical behavior.** Discipline options should be clearly communicated and consistently enforced.

An ethics policy will not be effective if it is handed to each new employee and then forgotten. The ethics policy should be reviewed with employees every year, ideally as part of an antifraud education program.

CASE STUDY: CONDUCTING BUSINESS PROFESSIONALLY AND SAFELY

Dan Fulwiler
Dan Fulwiler Murals & Fine Art
Nashota, Wisconsin
dan@danfulwiler.com
www.danfulwiler.com

Dan Fulwiler is the owner and artist of Dan Fulwiler Murals and Fine Art. He is a self-taught artist who polishes his artistic skills and knowledge by taking a variety of art classes at community colleges. His signature style is what he calls surreal impressionist cartoons and posterized portraits. Fulwiler paints murals, faux finishes, and more.

Fulwiler has been very creative and technologically advanced in what can be done with murals. He has created a Giclee Studio addition to his business. Giclee is a sophisticated printing process on an IRIS inkjet printer. It is capable of reproducing millions of colors with continuous-tone technology.

He prints original works of art or photographed images onto canvas that can be put up as a mural. It is the closest possible replication of an original work of art, and it lasts for decades.

For all of Fulwiler's technological advancement, he said his most valuable piece of equipment is his cell phone. He said that his clients want to be able to talk to him, not his office manager or his assistant. Clients appreciate an artist who answers the phone. It is OK to let a call go to voicemail when your hands are covered in glaze, but it is not OK to let every call go to voicemail, every time.

He said his next most valuable office tools are his scanner and then his printer. Fulwiler finds the ability to scan art and bring it up on his computer for manipulation priceless, and a high-quality, inkjet printer is tantamount to creating professional proposals, complete with sketches and color swatches.

In other matters on setting up your business, Fulwiler said that although insurance might seem like a waste of money because you are careful, never break anything, and never get hurt, the truth is, if you contract out your services for enough years, you will come across a situation in which you will be very happy to be insured.

Things happen, which is why we call them accidents. This is why we carry insurance. The simple fact of the matter is most states require you to be insured if you are in any sort of business, and most clients will not take you seriously if you do not have insurance. Fulwiler speaks from the experience. He fell off a ladder and broke his arm. Having good insurance saved him when he was unable to work for eight weeks.

Trompe l'oeil cobblestone. Painting by Dan Fulwiler.

Tell the World

"""Kodak sells film, but they don't advertise film, they advertise memories."

~~ Theodore Parker (1810 1860), Public Figure of Religion, Lectures, and Writing

As a small-business owner, it might seem that branding your painting business or yourself might simply be a slick advertising move. However, branding is more about positioning your painting business and yourself as an interior design professional in a positive light so your target market can see your business is the best choice above the others. When you build a business brand, it is not only about what you do — it is also about the benefits your customers will receive from you that they would not receive from another company. As a painter, it is also a chance to show off your style and craft your image. Your goal is to keep your customers coming back and to renew your contracts with them year after year. If a client is happy with your talent and professionalism with the mural accents you did in his or her kitchen, he or she is likely to call you back when decorating their future nursery or recommend your services to friends and colleagues.

A brand helps you organize the full range of your marketing and advertising strategies. It will convey what you stand for and who you are. An effective brand will encompass the whole business and will include a special logo that will be everywhere in the business: on stationery, cards, packaging, signs, and more. This brand also will fit right in the pricing of the services or products, customer services, and your business's guarantees. Mary's Magical Murals might choose to embellish everything with a paintbrush that leaves a trail of sparkles or stars to convey a sense of artistic magic.

A brand will benefit the operation of your business by:

- Building strong customer loyalty
- Bringing more credibility to any project
- Delivering any company message fast and effectively
- Hitting an emotional level with people
- Separating yourself and your business from the competition
- Positioning a focused message in both the heart and mind of your target market
- Bringing consistency to your marketing promotions and campaigns

Getting Started

How do you go about creating a winning brand that will help customers identify your business with everything that will make them feel comfortable and confident with your business? The following are a few suggestions to get you started:

- **Identify your personal and business values.** Begin to construct this by listing both personal and business values (honesty, quality, and so on). Then create a "value statement" for your business based on this list. Keep it short. The more condensed your value statement is, the easier it will be for you to recall. In addition, the condensed value statement might be the perfect phrase to use as an advertising tagline that will appear on your marketing materials.

- **Create a mission statement.** A mission statement is like a motto that lays out the purpose underlying your work. For example, you may want to define your mission as "creating beauty unique to you." A good mission statement is meaningful but still short enough to remember.

- **Create a vision statement.** A good vision statement will specify how you will know when you have achieved the goal of your mission statement. Setting targets for yourself, and then continually striving to meet them helps keep you working smarter and remain innovative as new possibilities open up.

- **Identify your starting point.** Where are you right now in relation to where you want to be? Write down some of the steps you already know are necessary to make your business dreams become real, such as taking the proper legal steps and securing your first painting job.

- **Describe your market.** Understanding who you want to reach with branding is critical, as choices of advertising, marketing, and other types of publicity will vary depending on the target market(s) you select. If you want to paint children's rooms, describe your market as being geared toward young families.

- **Create a positioning statement.** Positioning is your attempt to control the image of the business your customer will see. What is the impression you hope to make in the mind of your ideal customer? In your community, will you aim to be the lowest-cost painter? The top-quality artist? The most friendly, reliable painter?

Name your business for appeal and recognition

Ideally, the name of your business captures its essence. There are pros and cons for using your name for your business. When you share your name and identity with your company, you create a personal connection with your clients and your target market. You also use your personal reputation and community image to help build your business.

The naming process takes place after you have determined the structure of the business you are proposing. You will want to be sure the name you select is legal and accurately reflects what your business does. Verify that no other business in your area shares the name you are considering. You might have to file your name with your state or local government for approval. You cannot legally call yourself "Mary's Magical Murals" if you do not have a license.

Avoid long, hard-to-remember names such as Mary's Magical Murals, Faux Painting, and Decorating. You might brainstorm business name ideas with friends or business advisers. Think not only of how the name will sound when you answer the phone, but how it will look on a flier or other advertising. Reserve the URL or Web address of your website as soon as you choose a business name to secure it as your own before someone else does, even if you do not plan to set up the website for a few months. Also, you might want to check the availability of selected Web addresses by trying to access the site on the Web before you settle on a name.

While calling your business by the owner's name is a common approach, like "Mary's Murals," it is descriptive, but boring. You might want to go beyond the obvious. If so, it is fine to explore your creativity. If you are unsure how come up with a creative name, get out the yellow pages and look at the wide variety of names for hair salons, restaurants, or other businesses. Pick out your favorites, and then try to understand why they appeal to you. Ask outsiders — friends, relatives, professional advisers — what they think of your ideas, and whether they have suggestions. You want to avoid being too "cute" or unprofessional, while still being memorable and polished.

Develop your logo

The logo is a visual symbol of your business and your brand. There are many different considerations to keep in mind when choosing a logo or having one designed for you. You will probably want to keep it graphically simple, so it can be enlarged or made smaller, yet remain easily recognizable. A professional graphic designer might be helpful in preparing the logo for use in multiple formats. It should look as good on a billboard as it does on your truck, an invoice statement, or your business cards. Hiring a graphic designer might be a helpful option for a basic interior painter, but for a muralist, creating your own logo with your own talents and style is another way to give the public a taste of who you are and what sets you apart. You may even want to use a vignette or image from one of your own paintings.

You will also want to think ahead to the cost of reproducing your logo. Ideally, it will look good in black and white as well as in color, because color printing costs more and you might want to conserve costs at some point. If it renders well in black and gray, it will deliver that much more punch when you can afford to print it in color.

The combined effect of your values statement, mission statement, vision, and position statement, plus your definition of market, your business name, and your logo will become, over time, the foundation of your brand. Your unique "business personality" will be presented to the target market through business cards, fliers, brochures, online ad mediums, the yellow pages, and possibly newspaper, radio, or TV advertising. If you develop unified themes and are consistent in presenting your business message and image, your brand will grow with you as your customer list increases. People will know who you are and what you represent. That consistent, positive message will greatly increase your chances for profits and long-term success. If you are selling yourself as an artist, make your "business personality" eye-catching, stunning, or beautiful. It will show your artistic skills and eye for beauty to the public, which is the quickest way to advertise your talents.

CASE STUDY: DRUMMING UP BUSINESS

Jim Looney
Knoxville, Tennessee
www.adventureroom.com

Jim Looney is a one-man operation for creating hundreds of murals in Knoxville, Tennessee. With an education in faux painting that he has carried over into his murals, he has obtained contracts with clients with residential needs and commercial sites to be beautified, as well as area schools.

Word spreads quickly around a town that is being enhanced one wall at a time with captivating images of pastoral scenes, underwater-scapes, waterfalls, and more. This is how Looney has built his business: word of mouth. He said it has been his most successful form of advertising. It also works well for a single painter, as he said that there is only so much work he can do by himself.

In the beginning of his career, Looney placed a listing in the phone book. He never received any business from it, but he did receive phone calls from many salespeople and others who wanted him to paint things for practically nothing. This was not exactly his target market.

Instead of placing such a listing, Looney recommends taking an ad out in the smaller community newspapers in your area. He said it is a good way to get your name out there if you are new, and it can be a boost to your business if you can find a small paper that circulates within a retirement community.

Looney said that websites are a great way to advertise yourself if you get your site listed on a search engine. He said, however, that he only gets about 10 percent of his clients from Internet searches for a muralist. However, most of his clients visit his website to see examples of his work. He recommends carrying business cards with your website address on them.

30-second elevator pitch

Prepare your elevator speech (a 30-second rapid fire description of what your business does), and be ready to deliver that speech, with a business card, at every opportunity, including whenever you are in a public place, at a trade show, in the home improvement store, or wherever people gather. The more people know who you are and what you do, the more business you will get.

Using Social Media and Networking

Social networking is the new "it" marketing vehicle. The main objective is to allow members who have the same interest to interact and exchange information. Many small businesses are finding social networking to be a great way to build and grow, especially in tough economic times when advertising budgets have been cut. Instead of paying for costly advertising, you are spreading information through word of mouth and websites that are generally free to use.

Although the exact definition is still being clarified, social networking essentially refers to an online community or group of users where people can connect and communicate with others. Although the actual format can vary from one network to another, communication takes place in many ways including blogs, e-mail, instant messaging, forums, video, or chat rooms. Social networking connects people across the world in the privacy of their own homes, and the networking sites are usually free and instantaneous. Artists can easily post photos of their work, announce art shows, or use their network to sniff out work opportunities, sometimes simply by asking. There are thousands of social networking sites, some that are primarily for social use and others that are for business networking. For an artist, any networking site that allows you to upload photos will be advantageous. MySpace and Facebook both support photo uploading and ways to tell people about your business in as much or as little detail as you choose.

How it will help

Members of social networking sites are numerous, which creates an excellent opportunity for an individual to expand and promote a business without having to pay for advertising. With social networking, you can build an image and develop your customer base. To increase their website traffic, many site owners are quickly realizing the value social networking sites have in drawing new customers. The following are some ideas on how to use social networking sites to generate website traffic:

- Link your website to your social network profile.
- Create and share videos and photos on Flickr® and YouTube® describing your business, products, and services.
- Use social networking forums to promote your business, website, and blog.
- Promote your business through your profile, with links to your home page.

Popular social networking sites

With the ever increasing number of people who use the Internet on a regular basis, these social Websites have become a must, as this is the best and the easiest way for people to get connected with each other and stay in touch.

Facebook (**www.facebook.com**) is the leading social networking site, with more than 500 million active users at the time of publication.

Initially, Facebook was developed to connect university students, but over time, the site became available publicly and its popularity exploded. The majority of users on Facebook are college and high school students, but this trend is shifting rapidly to people of all ages and backgrounds. On Facebook, it is extremely easy to add friends, send messages, and create communities or event invitations.

MySpace® (**www.myspace.com**) is a social networking website that offers an interactive platform for all its users. It allows the sharing of files, pictures, and even music videos. You can view the profiles of your friends and relatives; you can also create and share blogs with each other. Users often compare Facebook to MySpace, but one major difference between the two websites is the level of customization. MySpace is a large social networking site that allows users to create profiles using HTML and CSS, while Facebook only allows plain text. The most prominent feature that makes MySpace unique among other sites is its affiliate program. If the affiliate product you are selling has a broad appeal, you might want consider using MySpace to market your product, as you will be able to reach the largest crowd quickly.

YouTube (**www.youtube.com**) is another social networking site owned by Google. To become a member of YouTube, go to the "Signup" page, choose a username and password, enter your information, and click the "Signup" button. YouTube is the most popular video sharing network site in the world, and it is a great place to do video marketing.

Orkut (**www.orkut.com**) is a popular social networking site owned by Google™. This social networking site has millions of users; 50.6 percent of Orkut traffic originates from Brazil, followed by India with 20.4 percent. Like other sites such as Facebook, Orkut permits the creation of groups known as "communities" based on a designated subject and allows other people to join the communities. Orkut is an online community designed to make your social life more active and stimulating as well as increase business contacts within industries.

Digg[SM] (**http://digg.com**) is a place to discover and share content from around the Web, from the smallest blog to major news outlets. Digg is unique compared to other social networking sites because it allows you to directly network with people and directly sell products. Once a post is submitted, it appears on a list in the selected category. From there, it will either fall in ranking or rise in raking, depending on how people vote. Digg is actually what is known as a "social bookmarking" site. You submit your content to Digg, and other Digg users — known as Diggers — will review and rate it. Once it is rated high enough, your content may get posted on the home page of Digg, which gets thousands of visitors a day, potentially driving tons of traffic to your website or blog.

Twitter[SM] (**http://twitter.com**) is different from other social networking sites, and the popularity of Twitter has grown at an amazing rate. With Twitter, you can let your friends know what you are doing throughout the day right from your phone or computer. When you sign up with Twitter, you can use the service to post and receive messages — known as a "tweet" — with your Twitter account, and the service distributes it to your friends and subscribers. In turn, you receive all the messages sent from those you wish to follow, including friends, family, and even celebrities. In essence, Twitter is a cell phone texting-based social network.

Flickr (**www.flickr.com**) is a photo and video sharing website that lets you organize and store your photos online. You can upload from your desktop, send by e-mail, or use your camera phone. It has features to get rid of red eye, crop a photo, or get creative with fonts and effects.

Friendster® (**www.friendster.com**) had 110 million members worldwide at the time of publication and is a place where you can set up dates and develop new friendships or business contacts. This site is a leading global online social network. Friendster is focused on helping people stay in touch with friends and discover new people and things that are important to them.

Popular business networking sites

The following sites offer businesses opportunities to network with other business owners:

- BizFriendz (**www.bizfriendz.com**): Make new contacts, promote your products and services, get vital exposure to your business, and earn commissions while you build your network.

- Biznik[SM] (**www.biznik.com**): Their tagline: "Business networking that doesn't suck." Geared directly to entrepreneurs and business owners, with a number of different communities.

- Cofoundr (**www.cofoundr.com**): A private community for entrepreneurs. Promises to help members build teams and network with other entrepreneurs.

- Digg[SM] (**www.digg.com**): Locate articles online about your business, yourself, or something of interest to potential customers and then post them on the site. You can also find articles of interest others have put up on the site for readers to rate.

- Ecademy® (**www.ecademy.com**): Provides extra tools to

build your business, such as networking events, Webinars on online topics, and the ability to locate members with specific knowledge.

- Fast Pitch!^{SM} (**www.fastpitchnetworking.com**): Reports it is growing faster than any other social network for professionals. Set up your own profile page and network with other businesspeople.

- Konnects^{SM} (**www.konnects.com**): Gives each member a profile page. Join communities, meet other members, and network with professionals with similar interests.

- LinkedIn® (**www.linkedin.com**): Connect and network with others in your field or who can use your abilities and/ or services.

- StartupNation^{SM} (**www.startupnation.com**): Active forums with a wide variety of subjects for businesses.

- StumbleUpon^{SM} (**www.stumbleupon.com**): Post any information of value and interest to others.

- Upspring™ (**www.upspring.com**): Increase exposure and attract more customers. Sign up for free and get a profile page, find and join groups, and increase your networking activities.

- Xing (**www.xing.com**): An active group of professionals looking for ways to network with people of interest.

Google AdWords for Your Business

In November 2009, Fox News reported Google as the No. 1 search engine in the world, taking in more than $22 billion in revenue, more than two-thirds of all U.S. newspaper ad revenue. Unlike many advertising mediums, AdWords does not require you to sign a contract, and it is customizable. This allows you to freely drop, change, and add to campaigns or individual ads in a specific timeframe — and with a budget that best meets your business's needs. With AdWords, you pay the $5 account activation fee, and then pay for the responses to your ad, which are measured by how many users see them or click on them. AdWords ads appear with search results when someone performs a search with Google using one of your keywords. Ads appear under 'sponsored links' in the side column and might also appear in additional positions above the free search results. It works nicely because you are advertising to an audience that is already interested in your business.

With AdWords, you can create an ad within minutes to respond to a competitor's price shift or a newsworthy event. If you find that you will be involved in an art exhibition, you can notify the public by increasing your ad instantly. If you find that another interior painting business is running a special, then you can as well through AdWords. If a particular product you sell is put on backorder from your supplier, put its ad on hold. If you realize that you have surplus inventory of a particular product, adjust your campaign to offer new customers a deeper discount that keeps them coming back for more. With Google AdWords, you have flexibility and options to quickly adjust your ads and campaigns to react offensively or defensively to the marketplace.

The ability to change an entire advertising campaign in just a few minutes is astounding compared to the lead times necessary for many other types of advertising such as special events, print, and broadcast

painting

faux painting

murals

"Life is a great big canvas, and you should throw all the paint you can on it."

— Danny Kaye

faux painting

Faux sky painting on entry way ceiling. Painting by Dan and Karen Dollahon. Photo by Steve Chen.

Faux finishes: French word meaning "fake or false." Technically, wood-graining, marbleizing, or other painted finishes that are replicating a natural material are faux finishes.

Venetian plaster: A surface coating product that, when applied properly, creates a smooth surface with both movement and depth.

Faux marble paneling. Painting by Dan and Karen Dollahon.

Example of Venetian plaster. Painting by Dan Fulwiler.

Red leather faux finish
Painting by Dan and
Karen Dollahon.
Photo by Steve Chen

Example of marbling
technique. Painting by
Dan Fulwiler

*Marbleizing: A faux
finish that creates the
illusion of marble.*

glazing

Glazing technique in living room.
Painting by Shirley Fadden.

Up-close look at
glazing technique.
Painting by Shirley
Fadden.

Examples of glazing technique. Painting by Gail Harrison.

Glazing: The process of applying tinted, but transparent, paint ove a base coat to create a soft modulated, watercolor effec

Tuscan vineyard mural. Painting by Dan Fulwiler.

Mural: Painted picture on a wall or ceiling.

murals

Mural in child's room.
Painting by Shirley Fadden.

Child's room design.
Painting by Shirley Fadden.

Bird mural on column. Painting by
Ed Palubinskas.

Mural painted on brick wall of building as seen in Cambridge, Massachusetts.

Mural in bathroom
Painting by David Kinke

X

Mural in restaurant.
Painting by David Kinker.

Old world
fresco mural.
Painting by
Dan and Karen
Dollahon.

*Fresco: An ancient mural technique using wet pigments
paint on uncured plaster. Fresco is a mural technique that
gives the appearance of an aged and weathered fresco
using contemporary paint products.*

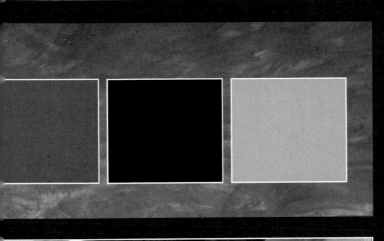

trompe l'oeil

Trompe l'oeil paintings in stairwell.
Painting by Dan and Karen Dollahon.
Photo by Katie Sullivan.

Trompe l'oeil statue.
Painting by Dan and
Karen Dollahon.

Trompe l'oeil: French expre
sion meaning "to deceive th
eye." A painting technique i
which an illusion of depth an
reality is created by emphasi
ing highlights and shadow

Trompe l'oeil cobblestone
Painting by Dan Fulwile

uilding: The application of metal in any
orm (gold or other metallic leaf, metallic foil,
etallic paint, metallic powder, etc.). Used to
omplement a decorative or faux finish.

Guilded ceiling with an
aluminum leaf with antique
gold glaze. Painting by Dan
and Karen Dollahon.
Photo by Steve Chen.

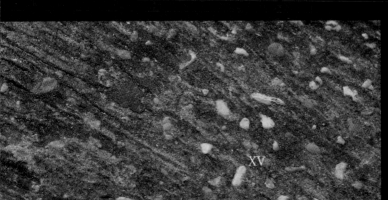

guilding

decorative painting

Logo painting on basketball cou
Painting by Ed Palubinskc

Painting on the gasoline tank of a Harley-Davidson. Painting by Ed Palubinskas.

XVI

mediums. AdWords is also multi-dimensional, flexible, and easily scaled, so that businesses and organizations of any type and size can use it effectively.

AdWords makes it easy for users to fully execute a single ad or an entire advertising campaign all by yourself. With AdWords, you can do a search for your keywords and take a look at the results yourself. It also gives information on Web pages that might include your ad. But it is easy to schedule your own test. Just do a search the way your potential customer would do a search. Go to Google (**www.google.com**), type one of your keywords — such as "mural" or "painter" along with the name of the city where your business is located — into the search window, and check out the ads that appear along with the results of the search. This is also a great way to check out your competition's ads. You can easily view the context of your ads on specific sites, news pages, blogs, or online communities.

Some of the specific things you can do with AdWords include:

- Create an ad that will appear on the Web
- Select where that ad will be shown
- Research keywords to reach your target market
- Set up target markets based on location and a variety of other options
- Use different types of ads including text ads, image ads, video ads, and more
- Set your own AdWords budget
- Bid on keywords that may increase interest in your ad
- Select your payment options
- Set up campaigns to manage multiple ads

- Analyze how individual ads and campaigns are performing
- Quickly and easily change ads and campaigns

Some of the possible effects of AdWords on your business include:

- Increased profitability
- The ability to explore new products and services inexpensively

Important key cost factors to keep in mind:

- The activation fee is a one-time $5 charge
- There is no minimum-spending requirement
- There is no contract required
- You determine how much you are willing to spend by setting a daily spending limit
- You set how much you want to pay either per click or per impression
- You only pay when someone clicks on your ad that is keyword targeted
- You only pay for impressions on your site-targeted ads
- Your ad position is based on the maximum CPC and its Quality Score

AdWords and your business goals

What does your organization's goals and objectives have to do with Google AdWords? AdWords helps you meet a number of your organization's goals and objectives — or just one of your choosing. While AdWords allows for increased revenue, it also helps you develop a human resources component to your business. There are job seekers who use the Web to find jobs locally, or who may be interested in relocating for a job with your company. Through AdWords, you might be able to summon a new employee to your painting team. Plan your business activities based on the measurable objectives that reflect your goals. Use them to make important business decisions. If an opportunity that sounds great initially does not match your business's goals, you might want to think seriously about skipping the opportunity or re-evaluating your goals. Remember to be flexible with your goals and objectives. Change them to adjust to changes in the marketplace, which may include:

- Changes in the number of competitors battling for the same customers.

- Changes relating to your suppliers, which could come in the form of cost and availability of equipment. An example of this would be shipping and transportation costs, which can certainly affect Web-based business transactions involving products. Your cost to ship your products to your customers directly affects your bottom line. If shipping costs rise, an AdWords ad offering free shipping might bring you more customers by giving you an edge over your competitor.

When you keep up-to-date on the latest technological tools that are available, you will be ahead of the game. You will also give yourself and your business a professional image. The last thing you want is to appear archaic. As an artist, one of the first questions you will hear from interested parties is, "Do you have a website?"

Painting on the gasoline tank of a Harley-Davidson.
Painting by Ed Palubinskas.

The Must-Have Website

> "The Internet will help achieve 'friction-free capitalism'
> by putting buyer and seller in direct contact and providing
> more information to both about each other."
>
> ~ Bill Gates (1955–), Chairman of Microsoft

Maintaining a website for your painting business is crucial. It will not only give prospective clients an easy way to find and contact you, but as an artist, it will serve as an online portfolio of your work. Most people searching for a business in their area will start with an Internet search. Give your clients information and a reason to use your services. This chapter outlines the basic components of a website, how to hire a Web page designer, how to use it to your business's advantage, and the fundamentals of search engine optimization (SEO). Remember to continually update your site with fresh information, new pictures, updated contact information, and new design features.

Website Design Fundamentals

The two most basic elements of a website are your Web pages: the compilation of HTML pages you have designed, and the images, content, and other information that will be displayed on your pages. Your individual Web pages collectively create your website. Your website can be as small as one page, or it can be thousands of pages. As a painter, you will want to have separate Web pages within the website with categories such as "About the Artist," "Contact Information," and a "Gallery." All websites have a home page. The home page is the page that site visitors are taken to when they type in your website domain name into a browser. From your home page, visitors can navigate your site and visit other Web pages on your site. All websites consistently change as new content and other Web pages are added, so while you may complete your initial design and publish your Web page, typically, your site will require consistent maintenance, updating, and revisions. The most challenging part of creating a website is developing a blueprint for how you want your site organized, what pages it will contain, how content will be organized, and how your pages will be laid out in relation others as you design your navigation and page relationships. Design your pages individually, formulate what each page should include, and then you can flesh out the actual content and site design later. You can do this work on a piece of paper or even with sticky notes on the wall, as this will help you visualize the layout. Be vigilant about updating your website with new information, and work to give visitors a reason to come back.

Four main components of a website

Even if you decide to hire a designer to create a website for you, it is a good idea to be knowledgeable about the different components of a website and their functions so you can be aware of every aspect of your business.

The basic components of a website are:

1. Domain name: This name is registered with a domain host, such as Go Daddy, and corresponds with where your website is physically located on a Web server and is also used for your e-mail accounts.

2. Web hosting: This is the physical "storage" of your Web pages on a server that is connected to the Internet. This machine "serves" your Web pages as they are requested by a Web browser, and this machine has an IP address. The Domain Name System (DNS) translates your domain name into your Web account IP address and serves up the appropriate Web pages as requested. Your domain registry will store the IP address of your DNS. The concept might be difficult to understand; however, it is actually quite simple. Your website consists of a series of Web pages. These Web pages are files, which are stored on a Web server along with images and other content on a Web server. This Web server has an IP address that is a unique machine name for that Web server. DNS servers translate your domain name (i.e. "www.mywebsite.com") into the IP address where your site is actually hosted and your Web server then serves your page to the Web browser of your site visitor. Therefore, it is critical that your DNS account (the company where you bought your domain name) is updated with the physical IP address of your DNS (provided by your hosting company). This ensures that anyone who searches or types in your

domain name into a browser window will be directed to the DNS, which then translates this to the IP address of your site, ensuring your Web pages are properly displayed at all times.

3. Web pages: These are the Web pages you created and published to your Web server. You can create Web pages with programs such as Microsoft Office FrontPage, Microsoft Expression Web, Adobe Dreamweaver CS5, and many other applications, including free design applications.

4. Optional items: Something a painter might choose to include is a place for customer testimonials and links to favorite artists or design ideas. Your needs might change over time, so keep that in mind during the planning process.

Hire a Web designer

A professional website can cost $3,500 to $15,000. This money buys layout, design, copywriting, programming, and the first year of hosting. Hiring a designer who is skilled, knowledgeable, or trained in Web design is a good choice for less computer-savvy people who do not have the time to learn how to do it themselves. Keep these suggestions in mind if you decide to hire a Web designer:

• You can find a Web designer online. Search for "Web design [your city name]" or "artist Web design" for people with experience designing artist's websites.

- Look at painting or mural painters' sites. Visit sites and take notes about what you like and what you do not like. When you find a design you like, contact the Web master. The Web master is usually listed at the bottom of the home page.

- Review designers' portfolios and samples. Do they grab your attention? Do the links work and do the graphics load quickly? Is it immediately obvious what the site is promoting?

Web design hardware requirements

You do not need to invest significant funds to be able to create your own website. You only need to have a reliable computer. Websites can be designed and tested on your personal or business computer, and you do not need to have your own Web server — in fact, you should avoid this cost. Many Web designers work exclusively from their laptop computers, which is a great way of having mobility so you can keep working on your Web pages no matter where you are. A minimum recommendation for a laptop is an Intel® Core™ 2 Duo Processor; although, you do not need the fastest model on the market. In fact, any mid-range processor will more than meet your needs for a long time. On the desktop, the Intel Core 2 Quad models are highly suggested because of the ability to effortlessly multitask.

You also need to have a fast, reliable Internet connection. It really does not matter what you choose as long as it is high speed broadband that is reliable and cost-effective. Do not cut corners on your Internet speed, and do not use dial-up because it is far too slow and you will become frustrated with its limitations very quickly. You might want to use an external 1TB hard drive for regular backups, while programs like Carbonite™ are extremely useful for full backups of websites. You can get a free trial of Carbonite at **www.carbonite.com.**

For graphics editing, popular options include Corel® Paint Shop Pro® X2 and Adobe Photoshop® CS5, which are great choices for the design needs of your website. Some well-known examples of Web design software include Microsoft Office FrontPage, Microsoft Expression Web, and Adobe Dreamweaver CS5. Other design applications such as Serif WebPlus X2 offer great tools for the novice designer. That said, you do not need to invest significant funds into advanced Web design applications. There are also many freeware, or free software, offerings for both your Web design and graphics editing needs, which will be discussed later on. Also, it is important to recognize that most Web hosting companies also provide easy-to-use website templates as part of your hosting package, enabling you to create a great looking site quickly and very easily.

In the Web design and development communities, you will see two distinct groups: the Microsoft group and the Adobe group. The Adobe group uses Adobe Dreamweaver CS5. Most Web developers consider Dreamweaver to be the professional Web designer's product of choice. In comparison, many used to consider Microsoft Office FrontPage to be the beginner's tool. Microsoft changed that with the release of Microsoft Expression Web, which matches up favorably with Dreamweaver. Microsoft no longer officially supports FrontPage, but it is still readily available for purchase. It is a good beginner tool that provides you with the environment where you create in design mode and the software writes the HTML code for you. WebPlus X2 is also a great design application for those without any HTML experience.

Domain Names

You must own your own domain name if you want to have a serious Web presence. Your domain name is your brand name on the Web. It is the address every site visitor will type in to visit your website, and it is critical that you choose a good domain name and host it with a reputable provider, such as Yahoo! or Go Daddy. There are dozens of companies you can purchase your domain names from. A good way to see your options is to do a search on domain name providers. Most offer convenient control panels that let you update settings including DNS server IP addresses. If you have your own company exchange server, you will also be able to change IP addresses for your mail servers if you do not wish to use the provided POP, or post office protocol, e-mail accounts with your hosting account. This will also allow you to update your contact information, name, address, and e-mail addresses.

Your domain name should uniquely identify your business. The general rule of thumb is the shorter the domain name, the better, and it should be relevant to your company name, service, or products. If you already have an established corporate name or identity, you should try to base your domain name on that corporate identity. This will allow customers to identify your company name with your domain name. For example, Mary's Magical Murals would ideally use a domain name of www.marysmagical-murals.com. We also highly recommend that you secure any similar domain names, the main reason being to protect your identity from others who may use a very similar sounding or identical domain name, with a different extension. Using the example above, you would also want to tab www.marysmagicalmurals.com and www.marysmagicalmurals.net. Your primary domain name should be the domain name that is "hosted," while others may be parked at no additional cost and pointed to the main domain name URL. This way, you only pay for one hosted domain name but utilize many domain names on the Internet, all directing site visitors to your main hosted site.

It is important that you name your website after your domain name. The primary reason for this is so that people know your website and business by name. CNN® stands for Cable News Network, but no one calls it that. CNN is simply known as CNN, and the domain name is CNN.com. While this may be a simplistic explanation, your domain name should easily relate to your company name so your "brand" or company name can be easily recognized or memorized.

Many professional Web designers recommend using keywords in your domain name rather than your company name. For example, the www. strugglingteens.com domain name specifically targets the industry of private schools and programs by using the keywords "struggling teens." Therefore, when you type the keywords "struggling teens" into the Google and Yahoo! search engines, this website pops up in the top spot under the paid ads. Your domain name might have relevance in how some search engines rank your website, so embedding keywords into your domain name may help you achieve better search engine success. If you can put "murals," "faux," or "painter" into your domain name, the better your chances of being found. Another option you may consider is to purchase both domain names identifying your business and those using keywords. Put your website files on the domain name with the keywords and redirect the domain names with the company name to the keywords domain name. This will allow you to market the domain name with your company name, which helps with branding and get the benefits of having the actual website located under a domain name with keywords.

Keywords built into website content and meta tags are essential to obtaining and maintaining visibility with these major search engines.

For example, some keywords that might be used for Mary's Magical Murals are, "murals," "painting," "design," or "artist." Keywords are not something you implement once and forget; the keywords must be constantly updated to ensure immediate success in gaining visibility and keeping your site listed on the first page of the search engine results. Few people look beyond the first page of search engine results, so if you are located on page ten, or even page two, you may never be found.

There was a time when domain names were readily available, but today, you will find that many domain names are already registered. Typically, there are variations of your desired domain name available, or perhaps other domain name extensions such as .org, .net, or .us. You can check the availability of a domain name by visiting the Go Daddy website (**www.godaddy.com**).

Search engines do index the entire content of Web pages, but they typically give more value, or "weight," to the content that appears closer to the top of the Web page.

Web Hosting

Web hosting is a service that allows your website to be accessible through the Internet. There are a few choices to consider, and you should find which one would be the best host for your painting business website.

Partnering with Yahoo! and Amazon

When you establish your business, you can also utilize the experience of an established e-commerce service, such as Yahoo!, eBay®, or Amazon.com®. The added benefit for a service business is that you can be paid for your painting jobs through electronic funds transfer. As an artist, you could also use an e-commerce service to sell your artwork. Keep in mind that while these companies do offer outstanding service and exposure, you will still need to spend significant time on your marketing efforts. Some website businesses mistakenly believe that using a platform such as Amazon will automatically help to expand their business. It might provide more visibility, but cannot be used in lieu of your own marketing and brand-building efforts.

There are several different ways to build a business with Amazon. You can start small by signing up as an individual seller and sell products without a website. If you expect 40 or fewer sales per month, you can sign up as an individual seller for no monthly fee but with a per-product sale fee of $0.99. If you expect to make more than 40 sales per month, you can sign up for a Pro Merchant Subscription with a monthly subscription fee of $39.99 plus a range of selling fees (approximately 15 percent) on items that you sell. You can also go a step further and use Amazon as your website template. With Amazon WebStore, you sell your own services, but use Amazon's technology to create your site and utilize the e-commerce services you require, such as safe and convenient shopping carts. The template is very easy to use, and you are given numerous widgets that offer different features you can add to your store, such as "sale of the day" or downloadable music. You can sell directly from your WebStore and by listing products on Amazon. The monthly fee is $59.99 for as many websites as you want, and the referral fee is 7 percent. With Amazon, you can be confident that you are using a brand that is known and trusted worldwide. When customers visit your store, your website will utilize top promotional vehicles to encourage buying, such as discount prices, free shipping, or bonuses.

Yahoo! Merchant Solutions is another option for creating and operating your websites. Yahoo! requires a $50 setup fee. Then you pay a monthly fee from $40 to $300, depending on the amount of sales you expect to make. You also have a sliding per-transaction fee of 1.5 percent to 0.75 percent, again depending on the number of your monthly transactions. When setting up your Yahoo! website, you can choose from a variety of designs. It is also easy to manage your online products. You can actually sell up to 50,000 products with your Yahoo! Merchant Solutions service. If you are only selling a few products, you can easily type them in to the online form to add them to your account. If you are selling hundreds or thousands of products, you will need to import each product from your Excel sheet to their online catalog. You can offer discounts and run promotions, as well as offer gift certificates for sale. Yahoo! lets you automatically calculate taxes and shipping and accept PayPal. The Yahoo! name is also well established and will create credibility when associated with your website.

Which service is a better choice? You will find merchants who swear by either Amazon or Yahoo! because one of these opportunities better fits their needs. Some vendors feel they get lost in myriad products on Amazon. Others appreciate the fact that their products are competing against larger sellers. Some e-commerce sites feel Amazon is too rough on its feedback policies and drop websites too quickly. Other website owners like the fact that their customers are judging them. Some vendors love the Yahoo! template's flexibility and say Yahoo! has many more design opportunities. Others say Amazon's layout is easier. The bottom line? Check both of these out very carefully, as well as other possibilities such as eBay, if you want to go with an established company. Also, remember that there are millions of website owners who stay away from any of these structured platforms and go it on their own. They like the independence and ability to design and format their sites as they wish.

Whether you develop your own website, hire a design professional, use a company offering a website template, or affiliate yourself with a major e-commerce site such as Amazon depends on the services you plan to offer to customers. Each e-commerce website has its own priorities and needs. Carefully review each of these structures and decide how your company fits into the parameters of these options. Then, study other websites selling similar products. Small-business owners are usually eager to help other entrepreneurs, so, if possible, talk to the owners and find out how their sites were designed. What do you think of the website design? What are the pros and cons? Is this site standing alone, or is it linked to a larger e-commerce business? What kind of marketing vehicles is the website using, either on its own or with a larger e-commerce site? Each option has its advantages and disadvantages. The platform you choose will not likely make or break your business's success — it instead depends on you and the efforts you put into your site. You are the driving force of your success.

Choosing your Yahoo! plan level

Thousands of merchants around the world have chosen to open Yahoo! stores in categories including beauty, books, clothing, computers, electronics, flowers and gifts, general merchandise, health, home, décor and design services, garden, jewelry, music, sports, and toys. This is also an option for selling your artwork online and any small local operating painting services use a Yahoo! plan.

There is a reason so many merchants have chosen Yahoo! for their online stores — it is easy to set up, use, and navigate. You can set up your store in less than 24 hours, even if you are not technology savvy. Perhaps more importantly, Yahoo! is affordable, offering different merchant plans ranging from $39.95 per month to $299.95 per month.

In addition to its ease of use and affordability, Yahoo! also commands significant traffic. Nielsen Online continually ranks Yahoo! in the top ten parent companies in terms of Internet audience metrics. It was only topped by Internet giants Google and Microsoft.

The best part is that you are in control of your Yahoo! experience. Through an à la carte setup, you choose what you want to spend each month based on the services you want and what you can afford.

Yahoo! services can be purchased individually or as a package. For example:

- Domain names can be purchased for $9.95 per year each.

- Web hosting with domain name purchase is available in a package starting at $11.95 per month.

- Full merchant service packages can be purchased starting at only $39.95 per month.

- Yahoo! offers a variety of online marketing services at different price points. You select what services you want (e.g., pay-per-click) and how much you want to pay for them.

Go Daddy

Another great alternative to Yahoo! or Amazon is Go Daddy® **(www. godaddy.com).** This host offers do-it-yourself sites or professional site builders. Photo editing and posting makes for an easy online portfolio. They also have various plans for your budget. It starts with an economy plan for $4.99 for three months to an affordable unlimited plan at $10.49 per month for 36 months.

By choosing a prefabricated template, you can then adjust the design elements, such as color schemes. You can easily upload your own photos that will create an ideal gallery for any artist. You can also jazz it up by adding music, videos, or flash animation.

Go Daddy is user friendly and makes the process of starting and keeping up with your account easy, with tech support that is available 24 hours a day, every day. They also provide valuable information to small business owners with their community library. It covers topics such as starting a business, marketing and sales, and minority resources.

Search Engine Optimization — Explained

While designing your website, you will read and hear a great deal about search engine optimization (SEO). SEO marketing is a vehicle used to increase a website's rank among search engines.

SEO involves developing your website in a way that will give you the maximum visibility with search engines. The more customers who see your products and information listed on Google, the greater the chance they will click on your business's link. Similarly, the closer your listing is to the top of the first page, the more clicks you will have. Understanding how SEO works is not difficult. Applying it to your site in a productive manner, however, takes considerable work. Website marketing has become very sophisticated due to increasing levels of available technology. With millions of websites competing for potential customers, it has become increasingly complex to ensure your website is found by interested buyers.

All Internet professionals have their own ideas on how to achieve high rankings. Search engines are often called spiders because they spread across the Internet looking for morsels of information to bring back to eat. In this case, it eats words and phrases, and it prefers the newest, most interesting food it can find. These spiders, or search engines, hunt, retrieve, and collect information based on the keywords requested by users. They are searching for the most relevant results. Search engine spiders, therefore, study the content of websites and rank content by hunting for specific phrases. They use two or more related words or phrases to garner the basic meaning of your page. Providing relevant, frequently updated copy with the right keywords and phrases will attract these spiders.

Always keep in mind these two words: fresh copy. Search engines seek new content. If your content grows outdated or you rarely add new copy, the search engines will overlook your website. Your website's home page alone is not enough to keep the search engines happy. Blogs or extra pages with additional copy attached to your main website are required to rouse the interest of a search engine. Most importantly, you need to integrate the keywords, or those special words pertaining to your unique product or service, into your website design, copy, and videos. Use a different title and description with keywords on each page. Remember, the title of the page is the most important SEO factor. Also, do not forget to include a site map on your website. The search engine spiders cannot index pages if they are not available. Site maps help search engines understand the layout of your site. Using these keywords will help you optimize your website and be listed on one of the first two search engine pages. Most users will not go further than this to find the product or service they desire.

While using keywords on your site is necessary for SEO, overusing them can have a detrimental effect on your rankings. When websites are stuffed with keywords, so much that the copy become unintelligible, search engines and customers know you are trying to scam the system. When this happens, the search engine spiders will stop visiting your site and your site will eventually be ignored, resulting in low rankings.

The recommended keyword density ranges from 3 to 7 percent per article. Anything above this, even a 10 percent density, starts to look like keyword stuffing. It is even more important to have the correct density in the title, headings, and opening paragraphs. You can find keyword-density tools online to help determine whether your keywords are within the correct range. If not, find synonyms or rewrite the copy.

Directories

Search indexes direct people only to the sites they index. Directories are made up of businesses that have paid a fee to be listed. For example, if you want to have your store or business listed with a Yahoo! directory, simply pay the fee associated with the directory and your registered business goes into a categorized index with other businesses having similar services or products. When a customer searches a directory using a keyword, the directory will only list those businesses that have paid for this service. The directory will not list matches throughout the Internet as with search engines, such as Google. When you list your store or business with both the search engines and the directories, you get twice as much exposure.

Some additional SEO tips

There are some basic things you can do to increase the chances that the search engines will pick up your copy. These include the following:

- Commit yourself to SEO. It is something that you need to work on at least once a day. The more you are committed to the process, the better the results will be.

- SEO should be part of your overall marketing plan. You need clear SEO goals. Develop an outline of how you expect to achieve your goals and at what cost.

- Be patient. After your website goes up, it will take at least two to three months of hard editorial work to get the rankings you want in the search engines. The smaller and newer your business, the more difficult it becomes. That is why you want to continually work on this.

- Put at least a couple of topics of interest on your website every week using your keywords, which are original and not copied from somewhere else. Search engines like new material. This also gives you an opportunity to write about any other information regarding your service such as your latest completed mural.

- Build your website with a number of different pages and more copy. This gives you additional opportunities with the search engines. On each page you have online, there is another way to use keywords that will be searched and will reach specific potential customers. You can end up with hundreds of content pages, each one able to be indexed by the search engines. Use the keywords that you find are most searched in your copy.

- Keep quality in mind at all times. You want strong editorial content that will be of interest to your readers and the search engines. Make sure the narration on your site about you or your artwork is clear, descriptive, and well-written.

- Construct an interesting website, and always strive to make it better. That means adding content of interest to your main buyers.

- Do not forget your site map. Those octopi cannot index pages that cannot be crawled. Your site map will help the search engines understand the layout of your pages.

- When you decide on your URL, think SEO. Keywords in your website name are quite useful.

- Use a different, pertinent title and meta-description on each page. Remember that the title of the page is the most important SEO factor. The meta-description tag will not help in your ranking, but will appear in your listing and encourage people interested in the topic to look for more.

- Make your copy interesting for your primary readers. Make it visually stimulating with emphasis on the beautiful images of your paintings. They are the ones who will be coming to your site and soliciting your services.

- You want copy that is different from other websites. This is difficult for people in e-commerce. Put some time into your descriptions of products, and stay away from the boilerplates from the manufacturers. If you put your keywords into your descriptions, you will be ahead of the pack.

- Use keywords as anchor text, which is the visible text that a viewer can click on in a hyperlink, when linking internally.

These tell the search engines what the page is all about.

- Send out press releases, but make them count. Send out a press release announcing your arrival into the virtual world. You should consider sending out others, as well, because they can establish you as a good media source for your industry. Just make sure that your release is meaty and covers a topic of importance. Then media, blogs, and search engines will pick up the news.

- Start a blog and participate with other related blogs. The blog about your painting business could discuss various topics in the arts or painting industry or serve as a kind of newsletter or journal about the projects you are currently working on.

- Social marketing is becoming an increasingly useful tool. Join the appropriate communities on Flickr (**www.flickr. com**), an online photo management and sharing application. It is a great way to post visuals about your services and your art. As a service-oriented business, use Yahoo! Answers to position yourself as an expert in your industry. Yahoo! Answers is an online community that allows users to post a question and get answers from contributors. You can establish yourself as a knowledgeable person in your field and converse with other people with similar businesses. Remember that this needs to be a two-way street. You are not using these vehicles just for your own purposes. You should become a contributor and support others who need reliable information. The same is true about forums. Just keep in mind that anyone can contribute to a topic, so it is possible to receive some misinformation.

Meta tag definition and implementation

Meta tags are a key part of the overall SEO program that you need to implement for your website. There remains controversy surrounding the use of meta tags and whether their inclusion on websites truly impacts search engine rankings, but they are still an integral part of a sound SEO plan, and some search engines do use these tags in their indexing process. You will find conflicting guidance on whether Google uses them or ignores them. You do need to be aware that you are competing against potentially thousands (or more) of other websites, often promoting similar services, using similar keywords, and employing other SEO techniques to achieve a top search engine ranking. Meta tags have never guaranteed top rankings on crawler-based search engines, but they may offer a degree of control and the ability for you to impact how your Web pages are indexed within the search engines.

Do not repeat your most important keywords and key phrases more than four to five times in a meta-keyword tag. Another thing to keep in mind is that your painting service will probably be specific to a certain geographical location, and you should mention this location in your meta-keyword tag, along with the words "paint" or "murals."

Meta tags comprise formatted information that is inserted into the "head" section of each page on your website. To view the "head" of a Web page, you must view it in HTML mode, rather than in the browser view. In Internet Explorer, you can click on Toolbar on the View menu and then click on "Source" to view the source of any individual Web page. If you are using a design tool, such as Adobe Dreamweaver CS3, Microsoft SharePoint Designer 2007, or Microsoft Expression Web Designer, you will need to use the HTML view to edit the source code of your Web pages. You can also use Notepad to edit your HTML source code.

Optimizing Web page content

Web page content is by far the single most important factor that will affect and determine your eventual website ranking in search engines. It is extremely important that you have relevant content on your Web pages that is going to increase the status of your website in search engine rankings. As a painter, the most important content that should be included is a gallery. Viewers will want to see your work to determine whether you are a match for what they have in mind for their home or office. Be sure to be descriptive with words throughout your gallery. The content on your website is what visitors are going to read when they find your site and start to browse your Web pages, whether they browse to a page directly or via a search engine. You need to optimize your website with all the right keywords within the content of each Web page so that you can maximize your rankings within search engines. You can use software tools to find out which keywords people are using when they search for certain products and services on the Internet.

Not only are the visitors to your website reading the content on these pages, but search engine spiders and Web crawlers are reading this same content and using it to index your website among your competitors. This is why it is important that you have the right content, such as an artist statement or biography and photo gallery, so that search engines are able to find your site and rank it near the top of the listings for similar products that people want to buy. Search engines are looking for keywords and phrases to categorize and rank your site; therefore, it is important that you focus on just as many key phrases as you do keywords.

The placement of text content within a Web page can make a significant difference in your eventual search engine rankings. Some search engines will only analyze a limited number of text characters on each page and will not read the rest of the page, regardless of length; therefore, the keywords and phrases you may have loaded into your page may not be read at all by the search engines.

Optional Website Additions

For someone who is designing a website to support a painting business, there are a few options that you might want to include in your pages. Customer testimonials are a great addition that will serve as a reference and a way to show previous client satisfaction. You could either pre-approve statements before publishing them on your site or take a risk and include a guestbook where visitors and previous clients can leave comments. By providing such a forum, you also open your website to complaints and negative publicity.

Another addition to consider is a form for interested parties to fill out. There should be a place for their basic information, such as name and contact information, but also a place for them to describe the project they have in mind for you. This is a good way for you to read what a customer wants and then take your time to present him or her with some ideas.

Of course, every painter should have an online portfolio of their previous painting jobs and individual artwork included on his or her website. This should not be considered optional but a necessary component. Clients will have no idea of your style, abilities, or skills without images of your work available to view.

Meet the Client

"I have learned to respect ideas, wherever they come from. Often they come from clients."

~ Leo Burnett (1891–1971), Pioneer of American Advertising

You have honed your painting skills while building a portfolio of your best work. You have your basic office and painting supplies. All your insurance needs are covered, and you have researched your area, created a name for yourself, and plastered it in every appropriate location in town, including the Internet. A ray of good fortune shines on all your hard work and preparation when you get that first call or e-mail from a prospective client. When this happens, you know that you have done something right. If time goes by and your phone is not ringing, take another look at where and how much of your business you have exposed to the public.

Timing Is Everything

Hearing from your first potential client is an exciting moment, but the first encounter with someone interested in you is when you want to start doing your best work. This is when you will make your first impression and begin generating word-of-mouth advertising. It starts with making sure that you keep your appointments. Pull out your wall or portable business calendar and write down the date and time that you set plan to meet with the client, and be sure to be there on time. Being late or, even worse, forgetting the appointment, could turn off potential customers, and it might send them looking elsewhere for more reliable help.

Be a Pro

Beginning a project with a prospective client involves showing up to the site that is in need of painting. Whether the site is a home or a place of business, you want to arrive looking like a professional who is clean, neat, and not going to be making a mess of the customer's home or office. It is advisable to arrive in the type of attire you would wear to a business meeting, because that is what the first meeting is — a meeting between you, the business owner, and a prospective customer. It is not a good idea to show up in your paint-splattered overalls.

Although you are your greatest tool, you need to bring more than just yourself when meeting the client. Look at the proposed project and determine what design techniques and effects are needed to complete the job. Have a handy carrying bag or backpack to bring all the essential tools for this first step in the process.

What to bring

Tools that are essential to help your project succeed from the beginning are those that help you get to know the space and the client as well. The following tips can assist you in knowing what to bring to the first meeting with a client:

- **Bring a camera.** Take pictures of the wall to be painted, as well as the whole room, to help you determine the client's color schemes and décor. These bits of visual information will help when you are back in your office or studio working on the preliminary sketch for the final mural or faux finishes. Pictures will help you match colors and serve as a reminder for what is needed to make a space look its best. Taking pictures from the beginning also gives you great before and after photos for your portfolio, which will impress future clients with how well you can turn ordinary spaces into something special.

- **Bring a tape measure.** Use this tool to measure the entire square footage of the painting surface. Knowing the exact measurements will help you determine the pricing of the project and let you estimate how much paint to buy. For walls with very high ceilings, measuring will let you know whether your ladder is tall enough. Taking measurements will also help back in the studio. It is a good idea to scale down the measurements of the wall into a smaller grid when making the preliminary sketch on paper or canvas. This allows you to avoid distorting the mural in the process of going from sketch to wall. It is a shame to begin painting a wall only to find that the sketch you planned out for an entire view of a football field in a little boy's room is too large and the wall is not big enough to accommodate the details that you and your client agreed upon from your preliminary sketch. On-site reconfiguration of proportions is tricky, so plan ahead by using a tape measure from the outset.

For example, suppose you have a wall surface that is 10 feet high and 20 feet across. The easiest way to shrink it to an appropriate sketch size is to measure your paper size for the sketch by allowing ½ inch for every foot. This will give you a workable sketch, which measures 5 inches  in height and 10 inches across. If you need a larger sketch, increase it a whole inch for every foot.

- **Bring a notebook.** This could be a simple spiral notebook. It will be essential for taking notes. Write down wall measurements, needed wall preparation, and details that you discuss with your client. Writing down your client's expectations will help you greatly as you plan your mural and give you a reference point throughout the project. No matter how good you think your memory is, do not try to store all the details in your head. It is a good way to get lost or start on the wrong track. You might forget that the client is interested in a monochromatic color scheme and begin planning, sketching, and buying paint for a mural with complementary colors.

- Have a calculator. This will be essential for determining your final price and down payment. You might be good at math, but a calculator is still handy and will look more professional than scribbled out figures on the back of your contract.

- Have an invoice pad. The client might write a check for the down payment, so you want to be prepared to provide the customer and yourself proof of payment. These can be purchased at any office supply store.

- Have a contract ready to go. Having official documentation of expected services and payments, signed by you and the client, is essential for protecting yourself should future disagreements occur. *For more information on how to write a contract and what should be included, see Chapter 9.*

- Bring a portfolio. This should be the hard copy of your work. It should be presented in either a binder or a loose, but professional, portfolio case. A binder that holds 8x11-inch images is ideal because it is easier for a client to flip through. Your portfolio will help start a discussion with the client about what they want. They can see your past work and point out what they like or do not like.

- Bring paint color samples that come from any paint store. These are free to you as a customer who purchases paint. Collect them all and have some basics handy to show your client to help them choose the ones they like. Holding the paint samples up to furniture, drapes, or flooring can also help you and the customer visualize and choose colors.

CASE STUDY: GAUGING THE PROCESS

C. Ashley Spencer
Owner of Casart and Casart
Coverings LLC
Alexandria, Virginia
www.ashley-spencer.com or www.
casartcoverings.com
casart@ashley-spencer.com or
contact@casartcoverings.com

C. Ashley Spencer is an artist with an entrepreneurial spirit. She owns two successful decorative painting companies. Her first, Casart, is her faux finish and mural painting business. The second is Casart Coverings, a product line of pre-made or customized wall coverings. They are scanned images of murals or faux finishes printed on a canvas-like material with a repositionable, self-adhesive backing.

She has built her business on talent and hard work but also by networking with clients, paint stores, interior designers, and interior design events. If there is a home show in your area, register to have your own booth, or just attend with a stack of business cards.

Spencer works closely with all her clients to develop creative ideas for various art projects. She maintains this type of relationship directly with clients, professional interior designers, and decorating firms.

Beyond asking the basic questions of new clients, such as what the scope of the project is, what type of room is it, and what their budget looks like, she gets her best information visually. When meeting with a client, Spencer brings her "Book of Ideas," a collection of magazine clippings, organized by color for decorative and faux finishes, and a separate book for murals from which they can flag ideas they like with sticky notes. She also brings her portfolio, as it has much more than what is on her website, and any samples of her work that is in a finish or color they request.

While giving clients time to look through the books, Spencer takes this opportunity to measure the walls and survey the environment. She looks at their style of home décor, their color choices, and how they have assembled their rooms. She looks for their attention to detail.

She also looks at the need for prep painting, the need for large furniture moving, and whether there is a need for a parking pass if the client is a business or lives in a gated community. These are all preparations for which she holds the client responsible.

Spencer charges for this initial consultation because there is valuable time involved and it helps to weed out clients who are not serious about having work done. Once she prepares her proposal, a commission agreement is accepted and signed, and a deposit is sent, she begins work on her sample boards. Once these are approved and the on-site work is completed, she deducts a portion of the initial consultation charge from the final statement.

Spencer advises that a balance should be maintained between the administrative side of work and the artistic application so that your mind can be free to create.

What to ask

That first consultation with a new client is a valuable time for the both of you. Some painters choose to ask for a fee for the time they spend on this initial meeting. It is valuable time and if a potential client is willing to pay for a consultation, it shows that they are serious about having the work done. Many painters choose to not ask for a consultation fee as a service to the client in an effort to attract more potential customers. If a home or business owner is undecided about whether to have the painting done, this consultation time is an opportunity for the painter to get the client excited about the project's possibilities and persuade him or her to have the work done and to hire your services on the spot. If you have arrived on time, brought the proper tools, appeared professional, and are excited about your work, there is a good chance you will be hired for the job, even if the client begins the consultation undecided.

This first meeting with the client is also valuable because it sets the course for the entire project. This is your opportunity to really get to know the client and what they want. Finding out what the client has in mind down to the minute details is essential from the beginning so that you do not waste time on a preliminary sketch that is in the wrong color scheme, style, or includes the wrong content. When you present the client with a small painting of what their room will look like after you have worked your magic, you want them to say, "That is exactly what I had in mind."

There are ways of making sure you get this reaction, and it starts in the beginning with a critical eye when evaluating the room and the client. Asking the right questions when you talk with the client also ensures that the two of you are thinking alike.

You can assume that most clients have some idea of what they want before you show up. They have thought of or seen something that has inspired them to contact you. They might have already done their homework and will present you with a photograph of exactly what it is that they want. If that is the case, it is your job to make what they want fit into their space.

To help a client convey what they have in mind, ask key questions to help get the conversation started between you and the client and break through barriers of vocabulary and ideas. Some example questions to ask for a home or office project are:

- What type of ambience do you want for this room?
- Would you like me to incorporate the color and décor of the room into the mural?
- Are there specific elements you would like me to include?
- What inspired you to have painting work done?
- What type of theme are you looking for?

Answers to these questions will be as varied as the clients themselves. Keep an open mind, and if you do not understand what it is the client wants, offer suggestions with photographs or sketches in the general ballpark of what he or she is looking for. This will give the client the opportunity to tell you if your interpretation of his or her answers are correct.

Checking Out the Site

All too often, clients will have only a vague notion of what they want, and it is up to you to help them crystallize their vision. The first step in doing this is to eyeball their style.

By observing the colors and style in a client's room, you can get a sense of what they might want. Look at the colors of the furniture, window treatments, counter tops, and flooring. Notice the main colors of these elements and pick out any accent colors. Determine whether their overall décor is modern, traditional, romantic, country, ethnic, or carries a theme. Using your artistic eye can help you determine things that clients do not tell you or cannot quite verbalize. They might simply tell you that they want to make the room prettier, which might be the extent of their artistic vocabulary. This is where your expertise can come in and help guide them by pointing out styles, elements, or colors that already exist in their room. You might direct their attention to a certain chair and say, "This chair has a shabby chic look to it. Is this a feel that you would like to carry throughout the room?" Or, you could ask, "You have some eclectic Asian decorative items, would you like to expand upon them and make it a theme?"

Sometimes, when you are hired, the customer does not know what he or she wants and expects your expertise to help guide the decision-making process. Be prepared to be an artistic guide. Become knowledgeable about interior decorating and various themes and styles, and then practice picking them out and talking about them wherever you go.

The consultation visit will also give you the opportunity to size up the job. During this time, you should measure the walls and look for potential obstacles and trouble spots. Some things to look for are ceiling heights, delicate flooring, valuable or breakable items or furniture, or walls in need of repair. These are all things to take into account when deciding what to charge the client and what the client will be responsible for removing or repairing. These obstacles can create the need to rent or buy new equipment, such as scaffolding, to work comfortably on rooms with high ceilings or laborers to help with large projects, and might require more time on your part. These can all increase the price of the project. Be sure to let the client know why they are being charged extra.

Stairs and stairwells can be a common, but workable, obstacle where special considerations, time, and equipment are usually required.

Obstacles are inevitable. Being flexible, gaining experience, and getting the advice of others will help you to know how to overcome them. Most troubleshooting can be accomplished with planning and communication of your needs with the client.

Client responsibilities

It is up to you to decide which duties you want to take on, such as moving furniture, and which duties you want to hold the client responsible for such as repairing damaged walls that existed before your work begins. In the beginning, you might be overly eager to please and, therefore, willing to take on tasks that most experienced painters hold the client responsible for. Try to remember that you are a painter; it is your talent and skills in this area — and this area only — that you are being hired for.

More often than not, a room will have furniture that will need to be removed in order to paint a wall. This is something that is usually up to the client to do before you show up to paint. Be sure to discuss your needs of furniture moving or removal of breakable or delicate items during your consultation visit. If the client is unable to move furniture, let him or her know that you will hire someone to move the furniture, but you will need to charge an additional fee for this service.

Some painters require the client to take care of all wall preparation, such as removing old wallpaper, filling in cracks and holes, laying down a base coat of paint, or making repairs, before they arrive. Whether you would like to take on this aspect of the job is up to you, but it should also be taken into account when figuring your costs because it will take extra time, supplies, and maybe even extra employees to accomplish. Also take into account your own abilities and experience. If you have a flair for wall repair and you do not mind doing it for a small fee, the customer might be grateful if you include that service in your job. However, if you have no experience in these matters, discuss it with the customer and give him or her the option of taking care of it before you arrive or paying you to hire an outside contractor to do it. *For more information on the specifics of wall preparation, see Chapter 11 and Chapter 12.*

If the client lives in an area with zoned parking areas, it should be up to the client to supply you with the proper parking pass. If you are required to travel a far distance to do the job, it is not unheard of for the client to be responsible for covering all your travel expenses. There are many muralists who operate out of their area and simply charge a fee for the expense to do so. When you become a well-known and respected painter with a solid reputation, this might become an opportunity for you as well. As your work becomes in demand, you might get requests from many locations.

The client's children and pets are their responsibility. It is a good idea to become friendly with everyone in the home, but you should not be expected to supervise them while you are trying to work. Ask the client to make arrangements to have them out of the way while you are working. You do not want small children dipping their hands into your solvents or animals running through your paint tray to leave their own artwork around the house.

Other considerations might be providing you with a security pass, keys, alarm codes, and contact number where the client can be reached if he or she is away while you are working, so you can come and go easily in order to do the job. It is important to present yourself as a trustworthy person so clients feel comfortable opening up their home or business to you. Provide references from other jobs so that clients can confirm you are as honorable as you appear.

The relationship between painter and client should be one of trust and clear communication on both sides. Having painting skills and an impressive portfolio is a great foundation to your business, but to be successful, you need to have polished people skills. Just like a doctor needs good bedside manner on top of his or her medical knowledge, you too need to develop a good "wallside" manner for successful projects and business relationships.

Come into all your projects with a positive attitude that will extend to the results as well as your relationship with your client. Keeping the right attitude can help with those occasional difficult clients. Just remember that you might encounter people who you would rather not work with. Some people can be too critical, too demanding, or expect you to listen to their life story, which can steal a lot of your valuable working time. Get a sense of your client on the first meeting. If you feel that they might not be good people to work with, it is always your choice to turn down a job.

Murals in dining room. Painting by Shirley Fadden.

May the Best Bid Win

"A verbal contract isn't worth the paper it's written on."
~ Samuel Goldwyn (1879–1974), U.S. Movie Producer

As a painting business owner, contracts will be an important aspect of the way you deal with clients and suppliers. Contracts can prevent confusion about how much money is owed and when the money is due. It will help immensely if contracts are written correctly from the beginning. Painting is contract work because each project you are hired for is a separate job. The contract signed by the provider and consumer is a legally binding agreement and states what is expected and what will be delivered.

Contracts with Vendors

Vendors provide the supplies, such as paint, brushes, and ladders, along with services, such as delivery, that keep your business running smoothly. Just as with every aspect of business, building solid relationships with suppliers is the path to long-term business success and profitability. If you earn your vendor's trust over time, they might be willing to provide help during those, hopefully rare, times when your bank account is squeezed. However, you do not want to rely too heavily on the good will of your vendors, especially early in your relationship, or overpromise your potential value as a customer to them. Mutual respect between vendor and yourself as customer is the goal.

What types of vendors will your business need in order to function? Vendors you will work with include local media or ad agencies that run your advertising programs if you create and buy advertising; a printing company that prints your flyers if you do not print them yourself; your phone and Internet service provider; a website developer; your health insurance provider; and the vendor who supplies you with the necessary tools to paint with. In the business of painting, you will want to develop a relationship with paint suppliers, your local art supply store, and your local hardware store.

Some of these vendors might offer you special commercial contracts for discounts on supplies or delivery because they view you as a fellow professional in the business. There are many advantages to arranging a commercial account, including discounts in some cases, but you might have to negotiate this with someone beyond the sales clerk to get your business plugged into the system. Usually, you have to supply banking and credit references, which are sometimes difficult to obtain when you are just starting out.

If you have good credit, you might be able to establish a line of credit with important vendors, allowing you to charge the goods or materials you need for your clients and pay in 30 days. This is a distinct advantage for you, because the supplier carries your upfront cost while you take care of the client. Then you get paid and subsequently pay the vendor.

A purchase order, consisting of a detailed list of purchased supplies and charges, is a contract you make with a vendor that specifies exactly what and to whom the material is to be given. There are several advantages in utilizing purchase orders. By officially giving notice to your vendors that you will always supply a purchase order for any charge, you will avoid mistakes that might permit an unauthorized person to wrongly bill a purchase to your account. Purchase orders also provide complete records of transactions with individual vendors so you can easily track how much of a particular product you buy. Because purchase order numbers are noted on vendor invoicing, all cost changes will be easily monitored. Even if your credit history does not give you the option to set up commercial accounts immediately upon opening your doors for business, you can still start your business. You should simply expect to "pay retail" until you can demonstrate to your vendors that you are seriously engaged in business and will be a profitable customer for them.

Another way many small business startups buy supplies is to use national credit cards, such as MasterCard®, Visa®, or Discover®. Credit card interest rates are usually higher than individual vendor credit lines, and the opportunity to build a close vendor/customer relationship is less compelling, but credit cards can give you the chance to make partial payments and not pay the entire bill in 30 days. Just be sure you pay the credit card company on time. Late fees involve serious penalties that will destroy your profitability in a hurry, while simultaneously damaging your credit rating and business reputation among vendors.

Contracts for Customers

Customer contracts require a different type of approach than contracting with vendors. There are several different ways to present your rates to your potential customer, including estimates and bids, which accomplish different things. A bid is a commitment to honor a particular price given particular circumstances, but an estimate is your best guess as to what the charge will be, though it is not legally binding. With an estimate, you imply "I am not exactly sure what this will cost." This approach is most effective when details are sketchy or you prefer to give a price range rather than a firm price. Estimates are usually expected to be given upon the first meeting at the work site.

You will also want to provide an estimate if your potential client seems unsure of exactly what he or she wants to have done or is simply "price shopping." If you would like, give an hourly rate and include phrases such as "a typical fee might be…" to retain the necessary wiggle room that allows you to adjust charges if circumstances warrant.

Conversely, a bid is a promise to perform a task at a specific price. Bids are legally binding because they are a formal written contract and are not open to change later in the job. You must fulfill the task as promised, at the stated price, or risk being sued. Large commercial or government jobs ordinarily require a competitive bid. You can expect to have many competitors if the work you bid on is desirable, so make your written bid as detailed and specific as possible. There should be no questions about what you promised to do or what the customer promised to pay for. Bids for projects involving a government entity, such as with government buildings like post offices, are public; your pricing detail will be seen by anyone who chooses to examine it. If a vaguely specified bid is accepted at all, it might be subject to questions or arguments by the customer. Some customers decide not to pay if the job was not performed to their expectations. If you have a contract, you can sue to collect, but lawsuits cost everyone time, money, and energy. It is better to take the time up front and submit an accurate, detailed bid that both you and the customer thoroughly understand.

Secrets of job estimating

Learning how to estimate whether a job and price is right for both your business and your community is the secret to a successful business. Ideally, you will get it right from day one. More realistically, you will make some mistakes and lose some profit while gaining experience in your new venture. Do not be too hard on yourself if you occasionally under price or overprice your services in the beginning. You will know you have overpriced a service if customers regularly go elsewhere.

Painters tend to charge one of two ways: by the square foot or by the hour. If you are confident in the speed of your painting and in your ability to quickly deal with unexpected problems that may arise, you might ask to be paid by the hour. However, this can create problems if a client begins to feel that you are taking too long on the project. Feeling rushed to stay within the estimated time of completion can also cause you to cut corners and not do your best. Therefore, most painters choose to charge by the square foot. It is a concrete way to show the client how much the project will cost.

One of the first questions a client will ask a muralist is, "What do you charge?" This question is often asked before the nature of the project is even discussed. Therefore, it is a good idea to have a standard scale that changes based on different types of work.

If you charge by the square foot, you can tell the client that your rate will depend on the style to be used. Give them common painting examples that the general public can understand. For example, tell them that for a faux finished wall that is purely texture, you charge $4 per square foot. For a mural that has little detail or cartoonish like characters, you charge $6 per every square foot. Tell them that for a mural that requires the kind of skill and detail involved in doing something like a reproduction of The Last Supper, you would need to charge $15 per every square foot. Then as you discuss with the client what their painting needs are, you can refer back to this pay scale and determine where their project will fall.

Keep track of what prices you estimate for which services and to whom. Also, note when you succeed in selling the job and when you fail. Review these records every week or two when you first open for business so that you can see what is working for you and what might need to be changed. Once you have gained experience, you might be able to let the records wait and review them once a month. To operate successfully, you need to stay aware of what you are doing, what works, what does not work, and what you might want to try differently. Regular evaluation will help you achieve this important analysis.

Create task breakdowns

Even if your customer winds up seeing a single hourly rate or project rate on the invoice, you need to track what it really costs to do part x, y, or z of any particular job. For example, how much are your supplies?

How much time will be spent on preparing a wall or a room? What will the preparation entail? What is the level of difficulty at this work site? Will it take longer to work around stairs, or will it be more strenuous because you will be painting a ceiling? One helpful way to track these costs is to do a task breakdown on each project. You might not need to go into such detail forever, but when you first open, it is a very good idea. This is a list for your own use, but it can also be shown to the client to help explain pricing if there are any questions.

A task breakdown is an itemized list of all the different parts of the job that will be performed for a given customer. It starts with the most basic task of all — getting to and from the job site. Tasks might include items such as prep work, setup and cleanup, and actual painting. For each category, if there is a logical overhead cost, such as supplies, make a column and write down your best guess.

If you are using an extra employee or contractor on a particular job, include the cost of these additional people on the task breakdown as well. The goal of your record is to compile a comprehensive view of what is involved on a particular job. It will also help you determine where you might be able to cut costs or when you need to get outside assistance to perform a particular task. At the end of the task breakdown, leave space to include what you actually bid for this job, whether the customer accepted the bid, and when you were paid. Save all of the task breakdowns from the first few months of your business. They will be a valuable reference source for evaluating what you are doing right in your business management and what areas you need to correct or rethink.

Bids you can live with

It is vital to create a formula that includes overhead and profit requirements for your painting business before beginning to quote prices to potential customers. It might not be a good idea to find out what your competition charges and duplicate that rate without determining whether it works for your business. Perhaps your competition is losing money. Competitors have different cost structures. Your bids should be shaped on the cost structure of your business — your overhead, your employees, and your profit goals. While it is important to know what your competitors charge for the services you plan to offer or are already providing, your basic pricing method has to be localized to be effective.

National average prices for services are of limited use to a business startup; although, a look at trends for the past several years might be helpful to see whether the work is likely to increase. For a general guideline, national average prices are updated annually in various publications. The U.S. Department of Labor also tracks information about a number of workforce and industry segments in its Occupational Outlook Handbook on the Department of Labor website at **www.dol.gov**.

If you have always worked for someone else, it might be challenging for you to calculate how to set the fees you will be charging so you can support yourself, your family, and your business. You can figure rates in a variety of ways — per hour, per square foot, or per project. It is important to be realistic about what you need to survive and what you can actually get from your existing market. Consider, first, the hourly rate approach. This will give you a realistic target to weigh projects and to evaluate your charge per square foot, should you choose to use those methods in actual practice.

To determine the income target you require, remember that as an independent businessperson, you must pay all your overhead, health benefits, vacation pay, retirement savings, and taxes. Total cost of living for you and your family, plus all business expenses and overhead, should be added together. Then, divide this figure by billable hours to determine the minimum per hour amount you need to stay afloat. If you work a 50-hour workweek, for 50 weeks (giving yourself some vacation time) that gives you a total of 2,500 work hours, on average, per year. Working 40 hours per week will give you just 2,000 hours total.

However, you will not be able to charge directly for all of those hours. You cannot run your business without setting aside regular time for marketing, maintaining equipment, and other non-billable work. Billable hour estimates range from 1,500 to 2,000 hours per year if you are working 50 hours each week. A quick estimate takes hourly rate x of 2,000 hours to project your potential annual income: e.g., $40/hour x 2,000 hours = annual income of $80,000. This $80,000 has to cover all those expenses you previously identified. If you want to make a profit, you will have to earn more than that amount. Also, to fulfill this goal, you will need 2,000 hours of billable work.

Price strategy and preparing bids

Successful service companies tailor their pricing to suit their community. Most communities will not fit the national average numbers precisely. The salaries and costs in your area might vary by substantial amounts, above or below the national average. You can always double-check your competitors' prices by doing a little price sleuthing.

You will find out quickly whether your fees are within the normal range for your area by the responses customers give you when they receive your bids. If every bid is accepted without hesitation, you might be charging too little. If you are being turned down regularly, ask customers why. If the answer is usually "too expensive," then either you are contacting the wrong customers for your business plan or you have priced yourself out of the market.

However, let's get past a great myth: You do not need to be the cheapest in town to do well. If you plan to run a successful business, your goal must be to keep your company profitable. Once you are running smoothly and making the money you require, you can donate your time and energy to those less fortunate. Until then, you must screen out customers who cannot afford your fees.

Your people skills are critical to succeed in this business. Look and listen, then repeat back to the customer what you hear to make sure you grasp the nature of what he or she wants. Pay attention to what the customer tells you, and read between the lines. If you are alert, you will probably sense whether this person will be easy or difficult to work with by the way he or she talks about previous projects or companies. This is more than "small talk." For future upselling, you will benefit by knowing what he or she wants in the short run and over the next couple of years. Ask what it will take to meet this person's expectations, likes, and dislikes. Write it all down, as completely as possible. Be certain you make note of any promises you give the customer.

Contractual Details

There is no one-size-fits-all contract for mural, painting, or faux painting agreements. The legal requirements of a contract vary by state. This is another area where you should consult with an attorney or call state advisers to ensure you are complying with state laws regarding such contracts. Each state has its own requirements on terms of cancellation, environmental regulations, and conflict resolution. Failure to comply can cost you money down the line. You have an obligation to yourself and your business to learn and comply with all of your state's contract requirements.

Some typical legal requirements of a contract include:

- **A Meeting of the Minds:** This basically states that the two parties involved with the contract are in agreement.

- **Consideration:** The considerations for the contract will detail points such as what service you are offering, performance expected, any terms or obligations on the part of you or the client, liabilities, and payment terms.

- **Legal Competence:** This will be the statement that each party is of age and of sound mind.

State approved, pre-printed template contracts might be available on the Internet or in your local office supply store, but make sure they are current. State laws change, and the regulatory agency in your state will not give you a break simply because you purchased and used outdated contract forms. It is your responsibility to comply. Your lawyer or the local chamber of commerce, state Department of Development, or Attorney General's office will be able to guide you to the appropriate contracting terms and procedures.

When a job is quoted, be certain you put everything in the contract. If the customer will pay weekly, state the terms. If this is a monthly or seasonal contract, specify the details and payment schedule. The point is to avoid misunderstandings. Customers always have a right to cancel a contract for nonperformance or, in most cases, general dissatisfaction. Consult your attorney about your state's laws concerning cancellation of these types of contracts and the rights of each side. However, you want to avoid producing large contracts with fine print, especially with residential customers. Potentially good customers could become offended or wary, wondering why you need all the formalities. Simply be specific, meet legal requirements, and do a good job. That will keep you in business.

CASE STUDY: HANDLING DIFFICULT PROJECTS

Dan and Karen Dollahon
Artistic Interiors by Dollahon
Designs
Houston, Texas
www.artisticinteriors.org
information@artisticinteriors.org

Dan and Karen Dollahon have pooled their talents and educational backgrounds to form a successful decorative painting business. With her degree in interior design and his experience as a draftsman, together they are able to survey any project — whether it is residential or commercial — and resolve the many obstacles that can come with owning a painting business.

They are happy to take on extra hurdles in their projects, such as needing extra equipment, moving furniture, protecting fragile items, or considering architectural designs. Each issue is carefully considered when pricing a job in order to give the client a fair quote.

When dealing with ceiling heights over ten feet, the Dollahon's will usually use a narrow set of scaffolding instead of ladders to make the job safer and easier. They also look at manipulating circular stairwells as an art form on its own. They say it can take up to four people to successfully apply the finish to these areas, by starting at one end and continually moving down and adjusting ladder heights.

If they are working on a ceiling over a circular stairwell and the diameter of the stairs is too tight for standard scaffolding, they have custom scaffolding built by an insured outside source.

Hiring additional help or purchasing specialty equipment can become costly to the painter and should rightfully be reflected in the bid that is offered and explained to the client.

Billing and Collection

The first rule of billing is: Do it promptly. When you are just getting started, cash flow is likely to be a problem. With small jobs, payment upon completion is appropriate. You want to invoice your customers as soon as the work is finished.

Most word processing software packages have templates for statements that you can tailor to your business if you do not want to pay for customized forms from an agency. All you really need to prepare a statement is a letterhead that includes your business name, address, and contact information such as a website, e-mail address, and phone and fax numbers. Type in the customer's name, address, and the date, and then fill in the details of what the customer is paying for and the amount due.

Finally, do not forget to write in the payment terms, such as "30 days net" or "Payment due upon receipt." Some business owners offer a discount for prompt payment as an option to speed receipt of funds.

In addition, be sure that you do not fill purchase orders based only on the purchase order number. Insist on a mailed or faxed hardcopy of the purchase order itself. A customer's employee could use a purchase order number without authorization by the person in charge. If the boss balks at paying for this order, and you have only the number, not a sheet of paper with the order specified and signed by the customer, you might have a hard time collecting. If, however, you have the detailed purchase order, it is a binding contract and the customer legally must pay regardless of who made the request.

When undertaking large jobs or orders, it is justifiable to demand that customers prepay 10 to 50 percent. This gives you some assurance that the customer is committed to the plan you have negotiated.

Bidding successfully on a project requires a balance of business sense and your ability to deal well with clients. Experience will only help further your skills in this department, but presenting your ideas well will help you win a client and have them primed to choose you as their painter. You can develop your ability to estimate and work with numbers to determine whether you can undersell your competition. This part of the painting business can be difficult, especially for an artist who might not love the business side of the industry, but winning over a client starts with showing them how talented you are and what you could do for their space. Once you have them excited, then you will have an easier time presenting them with costs and figures.

On the Site and on Your Mind

"They may be America's last pioneers, urban nomads in search of wide open interior spaces."

~ Cathleen McGuigan, Arts Editor for *Newsweek*

As a painter, your job location will be transient. The places you work will be as unique as the clients you serve. Each place will have positives and negatives. Some will have a deteriorating wall to repair, but lovely clients to work with. Some sites will involve a quick and easy paint job, but have obstacles such as lots of foot traffic or difficult-to-please clients. To be a painter, you need to be flexible and be able to "go with the flow." You also need polished people skills in order to deal with difficult clients, as well as problem solving skills. Experience always helps, but learning from experienced painters can give you valuable information, especially for the beginner.

When you visit a site to meet a client and survey the area and learn what their needs are, make the visit really count by looking for possible obstacles that could hinder your work. Thinking ahead can save you some time and trouble once you arrive to actually do the work.

Residential and Commercial Sites

Sometimes, you might obtain a job to paint the walls of an empty space where no one lives or works yet or where someone is trying to move in. These are the peaceful uninterrupted jobs. You can play your music, get lost in the painting process, and feel free without someone looking over your shoulder. These jobs might happen occasionally and are usually nice because there is an absence of the typical obstacles that you will encounter in lived-in homes and businesses.

While painting in a place of business, during business hours, there are a few acts of common courtesy for you to keep in mind. Never interrupt the people at work when they are dealing with their clients. If you have a question, wait until they are not with one of their valued customers. Bring all your own supplies. This goes for residential sites as well, but if you are asking the secretary for a chair, plastic cups, or paper towels, this can become a nuisance. Do not park in prime customer or reserved employee parking areas. Leave your car in the distance, giving customers the best parking spots. Also, never leave your equipment in the way of foot traffic. If you smoke, go outside away from the building and do not leave your discarded cigarettes behind. This goes for residential sites as well.

At commercial and residential sites, ask before using the client's bathroom or putting your food in their refridgerator. Usually, the client will be more than happy to allow you access to these things, but you should never assume.

Never set your paint cans, solvent cans, brushes, or paint trays on any bare surface in a home or business. These items should only go on your drop cloth or table.

Mural in a commercial site. Painting by David Kinker.

When you are preparing to work at either a residential or commercial site, you must take into consideration the client's space, possessions, and schedule. Ask the business if it is OK to work after their business hours. Ask the homeowner if you could work while the family was at work or school. This would be ideal because it involves fewer interruptions, but the choice is ultimately up to the client. It will usually come down to a matter of trust and the type of relationship you have developed with them. The client would need to provide you with a key and can only do so if they believe his or her home and belongings will be safe with you. You can help put their mind at ease if you come with references and always arrive looking professional, which will also give the impression of trustworthiness. However honest your face is, some people will simply prefer to be present while you are in their home or business.

As a painter, you will often be called upon for places under construction. You will have to take other workers under consideration and work with or around them. Try to arrange your painting schedule opposite that of the electrician who is trying to install outlets into the wall you are to paint or the light fixtures over your head. If new flooring is to be put in, it would be ideal for you to complete your painting before this is done.

If you are painting a structure that is not complete, make sure you have adequate light to see by and enough heat so that your paint will not be exposed to temperatures lower than its tolerance level.

CASE STUDY: TIPS FOR A SMOOTH JOB

Shirley Fadden
Wallflowers
Bellingham, Massachusetts
Wallflowersmural@aol.com
www.wallflowers.biz

Shirley Fadden holds a bachelor's degree in fine arts from Massachusetts College of Art, which she puts to good use in her creatively named business Wallflowers.

She renders murals, paints faux finishes, and provides interior design help for her clients. Fadden also does basic interior painting, and she said that when you come to a newly constructed work site — whether it is residential or commercial — you want to make sure the contractor is scheduling people appropriately. There are more people involved in the process and, therefore, more communication time is involved.

Overall, there are likely to be more interruptions in a commercial job. You need to consider the time and days your client will allow you to paint. Not every business is closed during a renovation.

When checking out a work site, Fadden likes to consider how the area is used and how much foot traffic the area receives. She said that a community room in a hospital might require a protective railing.

The paint will need to be washable and durable. In both commercial and residential jobs, you will need to consider the mood you are trying to create with your work. In medical settings, you might need to delve even further. For example, you might need to consider how a person with brain trauma processes color and contrast.

Fadden also considers the condition of the walls. She said that there is nothing worse than spending her time removing texture from walls that have been previously poorly painted. This can add a lot of time to the job. She also looks for cracks and holes in the wall. Older walls might not be smooth and, therefore, not be a good candidate for glossier paints and stripes. Shirley surveys the ceiling height and asks herself what type of ladders she will need. She also looks for any hard to reach areas.

Low temperature and high humidity can cause paint to dry slowly. If it looks like there will be issues with this, she asks clients to make the room warmer or she allows for extra drying time. Animals can also be a problem. If pet hair is on the floor, it is likely to wind up on the walls. Pets can also brush by the paint if they are allowed in the room.

If there are structural problems with the wall, Fadden points them out so that the customer understands that her price will reflect the extra labor needed to fix the problem. In her experience, some customers will sand and fill walls themselves in order to save money.

Fadden advises all beginners to document the time it takes to do everything required to complete a project. For example, you should note that it took one hour to unpack and prep the walls, four hours to put the basecoat down, and six hours to tape and paint stripes. This will help determine prices on future jobs that are similar

Setting Up

Before you pack your paints, tools, and other equipment to leave for a job site, do yourself a favor and make a check list. Check off the items as you pack them. This will save you the headache of realizing you left all your paint rags in your storage closet at your office 30 miles away, which leaves you with nothing to clean your brushes.

When you come to a place of residence or business, try to remain as inconspicuous as a person with ladders, drop cloths, and paint cans can be. One way to do this is to be quiet. Do not bring a radio to play music. If you bring headphones to listen to, keep the volume low enough so that you can hear if someone is trying to get your attention or a paint can spills. If you need to talk on the phone, go outside.

You will be expected to respect the property of others by being neat, tidy, and prepared to clean up any mess or mishap. If a paint can should spill, you do not want it to be on the carpet or splatter onto furniture. Avoid this by placing plastic drop cloths over everything in the workspace. This should be done before you transport any other equipment into the work site. Do not use fabric to cover floors or objects, as paint can leak through and attach to whatever is supposed to be protected. Cloths should be taped down to keep them in place and reach every corner. Remove all furniture and belongings from the room before you begin setting up.

Another helpful item to bring along to any work site is a small folding table. This can be used to hold the paint, brushes, and paint tray. It will save you from bending down to the ground every time you need more paint on your brush, and it will also help to keep you from stepping into the paint tray. Also, bring a folding chair that you can sit on and put you at the right height for painting middle and lower portions of a wall.

Do you have the grace of a ballerina, the reflexes of a cat, and the strength of a mule? No? Then be prepared to be careful. Even if all objects are removed and floors covered in the workspace, you still need to get through the front door, maneuver through the house or office, and make it to the workspace without damaging anything along the way. This is easier said than done when you are carrying large and heavy ladders that can cause dents and scuffs in walls or knock over priceless family heirlooms. Survey the route and ask to have breakables removed before you enter. You can soften the blow of a ladder during transport by taping or tying cloths, rags, or even bubble wrap to the legs and corners of the seat of your ladder. Just make sure these are easily removed because to leave them on when the ladder is in use could make it wobbly and unsafe. If you will be working in a room with wood or tile floors, bring along a skid proof mat to place under the legs of your ladder. You can also permanently attach the same rubbery material to the undersides of your ladder legs where they make contact with the ground. Some ladders are made with this protective material already attached.

Save yourself some time by mixing your glazes or paints in your own workspace before arriving at the work site. Make sure all paint cans are sealed shut. Carry potentially wet brushes and paint pans in a waterproof container. No need to get fancy; a garbage bag will do the trick and can be used for its intended purpose when you are finished with the job.

Another consideration is your feet. You will be going in and out to transport supplies, which can bring in dirt. You can remove your shoes every time you enter or purchase some disposable surgical foot covers that slip over the bottoms of your shoes. Put them on when you enter the house and take them off when you go out for more supplies. When you are in the room painting away, inevitably, paint will splatter on the floor and inevitably, you will step in it. Either paint while wearing foot covers and take them off when you leave the room or work in your shoes and put on the foot covers when you leave. Either way, check your feet and make sure you are not tracking in anything undesirable through the house. If it will not be in the way, you might want to lay out a drop cloth through your traffic area as well. Those paint cans have a way of popping open if they are dropped.

Be sure to bring buckets for water. This will be the most considerate way for you to rinse your brushes. Rinsing your brushes in the client's bathroom or kitchen sink will not only leave paint splatters and stains, but can also clog pipes. Rinse out your brushes in a bucket of water and wipe them clean with a rag. Be sure to bring one bag for dirty rags and one for garbage.

Even with the best preparations, accidents happen. This is why you need insurance, and this book includes a whole chapter on the subject. *Refer to Chapter 3 for more information on insurance.* You might cause more damage than you can afford to replace or repair. You always want to be prepared to handle the worst-case scenario when others are entrusting you with their property.

Finishing Up

Most painting jobs stretch beyond a single work day. There is usually several days' worth of work involved with most projects. You will have a daily and final clean up. When you are ready to leave the work site daily, make sure that all paint, primers, finishes, and solvents are in containers that are tightly closed. Clean and put away all your tools. Empty any water buckets, and take all the day's garbage with you. Do a preliminary cleaning of your brushes before leaving the work site, and then put them into a waterproof container or bag to take them home and give them a thorough cleaning. Make a judgement call as to whether to pull up and fold up your drop cloths. If you think there is a possibility for people to walk through the work site and step on wet splattered paint, then clean this up with rags or towels. Just remember at the end of your work day, there will be people who will be living and working in and around your work site. You want to leave behind as little as possible for them to step in, trip over, or spill. Always strive not to intrude upon the regular activity.

When the walls are completely painted, you are almost finished. Go around the baseboards and edges to check for any splatters or drips and take care of them before the client sees it themselves. Have some of the client's original base coat paint on hand for such corrections. You could ask ahead of time if they have some left over that you could use, and if not, match and buy some of your own. Also, check for missed spots in your work and take care of them.

Although your painting time has ended, your job has not. No project is completed until all your belongings are out of the workspace and the only thing you have left behind is a beautifully painted wall and a happy customer. Be sure to remove all supplies and garbage. Take your garbage with you and dispose of it yourself. Do not expect the client to put your garbage out with theirs. Make sure any splatter spill or damage is repaired before you leave or make arrangements to have it taken care of by a professional if it is beyond your skills. If you have spilled paint on and permanently damaged the client's carpet, you will need to have made arrangements to have it replaced. If there is dust or dirt on the floors from your work, sweep or vacuum the area. It is probably appropriate to ask the client to borrow his or her broom or vacuum cleaner, but you might want to bring your own if you do not feel your client would want to be bothered.

To show that you care for the client's home or business, put small objects that were moved back in their original place. You are not expected to replace large and heavy furniture.

To go that extra mile with a client and show them how much you appreciate their business, leave a gift and a thank-you note in the room that you painted. It does not need to be an elaborate gift, but maybe a plant, fruit basket, or knick-knack that goes well with their new paint job. Give small gifts for small jobs, but you may want to spend a little more on a gift to go along with a job that cost the client a lot of money.

Once you have painted, removed your belongings, made repairs or arrangements for repairs, and cleaned the workspace, it is time to collect the rest of your payment and say goodbye. Make sure your client is left with a few of your business cards to pass out to their friends or interested parties. Let him or her know that you enjoyed working on the project and to call next time he or she needs some additional work done. If you leave a good impression, you will be the first person that comes to mind when they think, "paint."

Eyeballing the Client's Style

As you are looking for potential dangers within the worksite, you can also use the opportunity to get a sense of what the client has a taste for, which can give you ideas about suggestions or proposals you can offer. Every space has a style. Even if the space is newly built and empty, you can get a glimpse of possibilities from simple things like the shape of the room and windows, chosen moldings, or doors. The structure itself can give you clues as to what the property owner has in mind. Ask yourself whether the architecture is modern, traditional, Victorian, or colonial.

As a painter, you will be a part of the interior design business. It will be in your best interest to not only develop top notch painting and drawing skills, but also an in depth understanding of interior design and the many styles and facets within that realm. Interior design is all around you. Practice by taking notice of what you see in homes and office buildings. Practice describing and discussing the style, color combinations, architecture, and décor elements that are in any given space. Think about what seems to work and not work in a room. Instead of simply passing through an office, take the opportunity to notice the elements within and sharpen your designer's eye.

Make friends with interior designers either through social networking sites or in person. Getting to chat and network with designers can help you better understand designer concepts. Introduce yourself to some of your local design firms. Getting your name and face out there in designer circles is always helpful to your knowledge and possibly a way to procure more work. If designers know you, they might call on you when one of their clients needs some painting work done or a mural painted. Interior designers, architects, and contractors are all people whose industry will be holding hands with yours.

There are many ways to brush up on interior design. Subscribe to home magazines and watch programs dedicated to interior design. These days there is no shortage of either, and they can help you keep abreast of what the current trends are and show you the many ways that paint helps transform a room or pulls the elements of a space together.

With a solid understanding of design, you will better your ability to enter a home and spot what is there to work with, draw from, downplay, and enhance through a coat of paint. For example, if you were to enter a room with small windows that let in very little light, you might suggest painting the walls in whites, creams, or light yellows to brighten things up. If a room is small and cramped, you may want to help the client picture a wide-open landscape on one of the walls to help the room appear larger.

As you walk through the room that is to be painted, notice the styles and colors of things that are already present. Take note of the room's window treatments. Are they a romantic lace, modern blinds, Asian bamboo, heavy drapes, or maybe curtains with a retro print? Play off of these styles in particular because the window treatments lay against the wall that you are to paint. The style can tell you a lot about the client and what would work in a room, unless the client mentions his or her desire to do away with the current style and add something completely different. Listen to the client's ideas.

Notice the client's choice in furniture, rugs, knick-knacks, paintings, or photos. Less obvious indicators of style and taste are mirrors and clocks. Taking a close look at these things can give you a sense of your client's style. These things might tell you whether the client likes light, dark, pastel, or primary colors. The themes and styles are endless, and with a background in design, you will be able to pick out and incorporate the client's style into your ideas and final product.

If you are hired for the job, use something in the room to coordinate colors. Taking a piece of fabric, a pillow, or some other small item will help when picking out paint colors for the job.

Sometimes, you might enter a space that seems to have no style at all. It may look thrown together and mismatched. If you can find a mainstay item such as a sofa or desk to incorporate into your painting ideas, you might be able to help pull the room together as a whole. The sofa might be a striking red that you want to tie into your mural or trim work. The desk might be a Victorian antique, which you might use to paint a mural with images of Victorian rose gardens or a period scene of people or places of that time. Look for what works in a room. Look for what stands out and needs some enhancement or complimentary colors to draw attention to it. By keeping these concepts in mind, you will not only be able to provide a fresh coat of paint or a pretty picture on the wall, but a space the client will love to live and work in. It will be a room he or she will want to show off.

Children's Spaces

Children might very well become your best customers. Parents get excited about setting up nurseries and like to make older kids' rooms an inviting place for them to play. They will want to create a room that beckons their children to spend time in them rather than the living or dining room. It is also very popular for institutions or businesses that serve children to make their space fun or comforting. The possibilities are nearly endless for this sector of the painting business.

Moms congregate together and talk. Painting a child's room is a great way to create word of mouth advertising. If you do a great job with a mural for a nursery, friends of your client will likely hear about it and might be potential clients. Always keep in mind that bad advertising tends to spread more quickly than good advertising. With each job, no matter how small, you are creating your reputation and influencing future work opportunities.

Pediatric offices are great places to find mural painting work. Better yet, if you could find a pediatric complex or children's hospital, then one job could easily turn into many. This is also true for working in a school. Many schools have murals in their entryways if not throughout the entire building. If you can make one school happy with your work, it is likely your services will be called upon throughout the entire school district.

The themes, styles, and motifs that are attractive to children are as endless as the children themselves. Painting for children can be lucrative and lots of fun, but it should be taken as seriously as you would a mural for a grand ballroom.

Being called upon to paint a nursery usually means the parent will already have an idea of what colors or themes he or she wants for the little one. Your job is to help parents realize the possibilities of their vision. Providing a preliminary sketch will help put you and the client on the same page.

Schools often want to incorporate the school mascot or colors into a mural, which simply involves rendering it in a style that you are capable of and the client will be happy with.

Example of a mural in a child's room. Painting by Shirley Fadden.

If the client does not have a previously concocted notion of what he or she wants on the walls, there are plenty of places to get ideas and inspiration. Children's books can provide inspiration for themes and images that a child would love. There is over a hundred years of history in children's book illustrations. Styles have changed throughout certain periods, but even older books can inspire a certain vintage beauty that can be used to create a look and feel of elegance. Take some time to look through the children's section in your local library. It will be a resource for children's favorites old and new. Again, keep in mind copyright infringements on the newer characters and book illustrations for any major or highly public project. You can also browse though parenting magazines for design ideas, especially if you want to keep up on the latest trends and styles for children. Interior design magazines also address décor for children.

Example of painting in a child's room. Painting by Shirley Fadden.

Scenes for a children's space do not need to come from a copy of art that has already been made. These jobs are a great place to use your own creative talents and imagination to create something original. You will need a good line of communication with the parents and their children if they are old enough to express likes and dislikes. Children have various interests. Some are more common than others. These days, many young children want either SpongeBob or Dora the Explorer to stare at day and night. Some little ones have more personal interests in mind. Bugs, fairies, jungle scenes, horses, farms, woodland creatures, football, soccer, outer space, castles and dragons, pirates, under the sea, cars, circus, musical instruments, ballet, robots, airplanes, and cowboys are all popular themes for children.

Be prepared to ask the parent about the child's interests. Find out which games or sports he or she enjoys, books he or she likes to read, and toys are his or her favorite. The answers to these questions will help you to put some options on the table and develop a preliminary sketch. Sometimes children and their parents will not agree on what should go in the room.

You can sometimes offer ideas that compromise the two opposing viewpoints, but these are matters that you need to let them settle between themselves. Remember, the parent will always have the final say.

Painting for children is a sector of the painting industry with endless possibilities. It might even be one that you want to specialize in at a future date. There are many opportunities for work and to stretch your creative skills.

Interior Painting: The Basis for All Painting

"First master the fundamentals."

~ Larry Bird (1956–), Former American Professional Basketball Player

Many people simply enjoy the act of painting. They like the meditative activity involved and to see the results after putting a new face on a tired wall. As an interior painter, faux painter, or muralist, you might be one of those people. Whichever you are, this is a good chapter to study, as it covers the "this and thats" of paint, tools, finishes and solvents, and safety, which are all topics that any painter should become very familiar with.

Lucrative Art for Every Painter

In just about every building you enter, there are painted walls. Homes, businesses, schools, government buildings, and apartment complexes all have walls that need a fresh coat of paint approximately every five years, depending on the amount of wear and tear. It might be a basic white or something a little more color coordinated, but someone had to put all that paint there, and someone was paid to do it.

There are many opportunities to find work as a basic interior painter. Although job opportunities for painters might slow down during the winter, basic interior painters might never run out of work because even existing structures need new paint every so often. As opposed to mural or decorative painting, basic interior painting is more of a necessity to a structure than a faux brick wall or a landscape scene, for example. It is also the kind of industry that just about anyone can enter. As long as you are physically able to do the work, which requires long hours on your feet and some arm strength, almost anyone can succeed in this industry. You do not need to have drawing or rendering skills. Even if you are a decorative painter, you might want to consider incorporating basic painting into your services because it can help fill in the gaps when decorative work is absent.

Tools and Equipment

Basic interior painting requires basic equipment that you can find at any home improvement store, or online supplier websites can sometimes give you a better rate than direct retail, especially if you buy in bulk. Try ThePaintStore.com (**www.thepaintstore.com**) for wholesale prices or H&H Purchasing Services (**www.hhpurchasing. com**) for discount paint and supplies. If you are not starting your business from scratch but are buying into a franchise, there might be a standard list of equipment for you to acquire that might need to be a certain brand or style.

Beyond paint, you will need to arm yourself with some reliable and reusable tools. Your vehicle will be your greatest tool, as it would be nearly impossible to transport all the necessary equipment to various job sites on foot, by bike, or through public transportation. Have a car, or better yet a truck or van, that is kept in good condition that you can count on to get you to the job site. Again, with a franchise, there will be a standard vehicle type and color with their logo.

Whichever make and model vehicle you choose, make sure it can transport your ladders. You will need at least one step ladder and one extension ladder. Unless you choose a full-sized van, you will need to make your vehicle accommodating to ladders by purchasing and installing a ladder rack. Ladder racks come in many varieties from simple one ladder carriers to models that can hold multiple ladders. The prices for a rack can range anywhere from about $150 to $550. To get an idea of what is available or to make a purchase, visit U.S. Rack (**www.usrack.com**).

All other items, though smaller, will take up a lot of space in your vehicle. Among your basic tools will be small to large brushes, rollers, paint trays, plastic drop cloths, and masking tape for edges. You might even look into purchasing a paint sprayer. Besides tools for laying down paint, you will also need some for making minor repairs and prepping the walls. The list of these items includes a caulk gun, scrapers, putty knives, a sanding block, and razors. You will also want a supply of rags for cleaning up spills or drying brushes and flathead screwdrivers, which come in handy for a variety of things such as opening paint cans.

Although you will be taping off many edges with masking tape, this is not recommended for the bottom edge where paint can drip downward, accumulate, and seep under the tape. All too often, by the time you pull up the tape at the end of the day, any seepage has already dried on the molding. To avoid this, use a paint shield. They are inexpensive edging tools that have a long blade to cover the bottom molding, keep clean lines, and prevent hidden seepage. These are also good for keeping clean lines in other locations of the wall as well.

For your own comfort and personal protection, it is also recommended that you invest in a few more items. Respirators are used as a shield against toxins in the work environment and should be used when dealing with the fumes of oil-based paints that can cause birth defects in unborn infants and brain damage in adults. It is also very useful when removing lead paint, which sends tiny lead particles into the air, or working with any other toxic substances that you would not want to inhale. Buy one that is approved by the National Institute of Occupational Safety and Health (NIOSH). You can shop for one online at Northern Tool + Equipment (**www.northerntool.com**), where they can be purchased for approximately $25 to $30. Also, find a good pair of goggles to use while you are dealing with toxic substances, such as lead paint, that will not impair your vision. Lastly, for your own comfort, buy a pair of knee pads. They are a hard plastic covering that will protect your knees from bruising and discomfort while doing the lower parts of walls, doors, windows, and trim work along the floor. Your knees will thank you.

Primer

Before you begin laying down that perfectly picked color of paint on a wall, ask yourself what kind of surface are you about to work on. If it is a bare drywall, wood, concrete, or even metal, it first needs to be protected with a primer. Primers are latex or oil based and unlike paint in that they have different ingredients that will seal the surface, protect it from water, and help create a flat and even toned surface to lay your paint on. Without a primer, moisture can seep through a coat of paint creating problems in the drywall such as mold, rusting, or warping. If the surface is porous, the paint itself is at risk of puckering and will soon begin to peel.

CASE STUDY: APPEALING TO AFFLUENT CLIENTS

Randy Ganther
Owner of Platinum Painting, LLC
Eau Claire, Wisconsin
123positiveg@charter.net
www.123positiveg.com

Randy Ganther is owner of Platinum Painting, LLC, which offers both basic interior painting as well as faux finishes for a target market of affluent clients. By networking with other painters and attending classes on faux finishing, Ganther has gained the skills and knowledge to provide an excellent service to clients who expect the best and are willing to pay for it.

He starts with a very detailed contract that covers all aspects of his services, including how extras, such as if a pet or child damages the paint while the project is in progress, are handled. During his jobs, he writes down what he does each hour so no one can dispute how his time was spent. His log is always available for the clients to look at if they feel they were overcharged in any manner.

He documents the temperature, approximate humidity, and general weather during the time he makes any paint or product application, especially when working on exterior project. When he is done with a job, he provides a work summary for the client.

This includes the exact paint brand, name, formula, and sheen. It includes anything he ran into that was out of the ordinary as a reference in case there is a problem in the future. He also leaves touch-up paint to fix marks that might occur in the future.

Ganther said that everything has a price, and tools are out there to solve any problem. He does require clients to pay for the extra time and tools needed to resolve problems.

Prior to his arrival clients should remove all breakables from the room, and all furniture should be moved at least four feet from the wall. He takes care of the removal of light fixtures and outlet covers.

He charges for any extra prep time that he needs to put in, such as time spent tying back and covering shrubberies on outside jobs in order to protect them from paint and chemicals. These things are always stated in his proposals.

The first thing Ganther does when setting up for a job is bring in large, clean tarps to set all the gear on. He always wears booties from the tarp to any flooring of the house. He sets up a main station to work from in as much of an out of the way area as possible. This area remains there the entire time he is working, and he covers this with clean tarps at the end of each day to minimize the eyesore for the homeowner. Upon completing each room, he cleans, leaving the space better than it was when he arrived. He vacuums the entire carpeted areas and dust mops the hard flooring areas in the rooms that he has worked in.

Ganther said that knowing your target market allows you to tailor your advertising language and the places you advertise to the people you want to reach. He likes to focus on affluent clients with historic homes. It means less individual jobs and a lot more money for specific equipment, but some years, he only needs one client in order to pay his bills. When doing rental re-paints, there will be a lot more jobs, and much less equipment, but they will be lower paying.

Ganther said that you should pick the area you want to work in. "A lot of people say they want the higher-end stuff, but if you are not neat, responsible, prompt, courteous, and meticulous, this isn't your niche – unless you become those things. Do what you are comfortable with, and you will be happy."

Paints

The two most common types of house paint are water- and oil-based. Water-based paints have water as a main ingredient, and these types include latex, acrylic, and vinyl. The differences between the three types is in their binders and what they are comprised of. Latex paint was originally made with rubber latex binders, but is now a mix of chemicals that retain the same type of plasticity and ability to expand and contract when the weather changes. Alkyd is the name used for oil-based paint because, historically, it contained linseed oil, but is now made up of mineral spirits. Many painters swear by oil paints, especially for murals and faux finishes. The result has a creamier finish than acrylic or latex paints. Latex is the most popularly used paint, and it has its benefits and drawbacks. Latex cannot withstand freezing and should be applied at 50 degrees Fahrenheit or above to avoid the appearance of brushstrokes. It is a quick-drying and odor-free paint that can be cleaned up while wet with a little water and a rag. The oil-based alkyd is used for its ability to hide brushstrokes and works the best in a sprayer. For these reasons, sometimes painters opt for this paint, despite its strong odor and slow drying time.

Sheens or Finishes

When going over the paint options with a client, you will have more for them to choose from than color alone. There are different sheens, which describe the glossiness of the paint. Different sheens should be used for different places or objects. It is important for you as a painter to become familiar with the various sheens so that you can help direct your client toward the right choice for their walls, doors, window frames, and more. The following is a list and brief description of each:

- **Flat:** This sheen has a matte finish, meaning that it is non-reflective. It is great for hiding imperfections in a surface such as scratches or dents in walls. Usually, this is the choice of finish for bedrooms, living rooms, or rooms that will not be exposed to stains or too much humidity.

- **Eggshell or satin:** This type has a slightly more reflective or shiny quality than flat paints. It is a great choice for places such as kitchens or bathrooms because it is more resistant to stains and can withstand repeated washing. It also repels water and has a better resistance to the sun, so it is also a great choice for outdoor paint jobs. With its slightly shiny quality, it tends to enhance any imperfections in a wall — more so than a flat finish.

- **Semi-gloss:** This sheen is semi glossy, which is great for trim work or around doors and windows because glossy paint better shows curves and indentations. However, it also shows imperfections in the wall surface clearly, which is not something homeowners want. Semi-gloss also holds up well to repeated cleaning.

- **Gloss:** This paint will give trim work and other objects the look of being made of plastic. It has the shiniest sheen and the highest stain resistance of all the other sheens. Any wall surface imperfection will be amplified with a gloss finish.

Types of Finishes

The finishing coat protects and adds depth to your work. The type of finish you choose could make all the difference in the world. A few choices in finishes are:

- **Water soluble:** This finish is odor free and will dry quickly, but it can require more than one coat to do the job. It is also not a good choice for placing over dark paint, as it can darken and tint your colors.

- **Paint thinner soluble:** There are quick- and slow-drying varieties to choose from, and the general rule of thumb is that the longer a finish takes to dry, the better it is at hiding brush strokes. If you want a smooth finish, use a slow-drying paint thinner soluble finish. However, this type of finish can yellow over time.

- **Shellac:** This is an alcohol-soluble finish that can easily be affected by and removed by alcohol. It is not the best choice for rooms such as kitchens and bathrooms, as it is easily affected by water and heat. This is a better choice for bedrooms or living rooms.

Paint Strippers

At times, you will need to remove old paint before putting on a new coat. Sometimes, this is because there are layers of uneven paint and globs that interfere with the final look of a paint job. If the paint is peeling, scraping and sanding can usually take care of the rest. If you are in need of something tougher to remove the paint you have a few choices, which are:

- **Liquid strippers:** Beware! These are highly caustic and can cause chemical burns. Although they are the most effective at removing paint, always wear protective gear and clothing when using a liquid stripper.

- **Stripping papers:** For a safer, less chemically induced mess, use these. They are best described as one-sided sticky tape that can be laid on top of the paint and then peeled up. Papers have the ability to peel off multiple layers of old paint.

- **Heat gun:** This is a great non-chemical choice if you are trying to remove a single layer of paint. It does not work as well on multiple layers. This is a great choice if you are nervous about working with toxic chemicals.

Safety and Lead Paint

A respirator should be used when using oil-based paint and while removing lead paint. Paint containing lead was commonly used until the 1970s. Lead paint was removed from the market because it proved to have negative neurological effects on young children and pregnant women. Many older structures have a layer of lead paint, which, over time, chips and disperses lead into the environment. It is dangerous to children, pets, and pregnant women. You may be called upon to remove such paint, and if you do, you need to take precautions.

First, keep all children, animals, and pregnant women out of the area until after the removal of the lead paint and final cleanup are complete. Work in one room at a time and keep it sealed off. Remove or cover all items in two sheets of plastic that is sealed down with duct tape. Wear disposable clothing, goggles, and a respirator. Do not eat, drink, or smoke while working to avoid ingesting lead particles.

At the end of each day, mist all areas with water, sweep, and then mop. Put all clothing in a plastic bag and either throw them away or wash the clothing thoroughly. Then, wet dust all surfaces.

When the removal of the lead paint is complete, vacuum all surfaces, including walls, with a high efficiency particulate air (HEPA) vacuum cleaner, including your clothing. Then mop and vacuum again.

Lead should be taken very seriously to prevent health problems for you, your family, and the people living or working in the area. Check your state's health department website for any state enforced regulations when dealing with lead paint. For more information on lead paint, visit **www.epa.gov/lead** or **www.cpsc.gov/cpscpub/pubs/5054.html**.

Finding Clients

There is painting work to be had; the key is to make sure you are the one doing it. There are different approaches to finding your first clients, and once you have done an excellent job for them, word of mouth advertising will help you along. In the meantime, start by placing an ad.

Write a simple ad for your local newspaper. Include your company's name and phone number, your services, and motto, and if you are insured or bonded, you should mention that as well. The words "free estimates" are always eye-catching. You could even include a logo or graphic to attract the reader's eye. You could run your ad in more than one area newspaper as well as any local magazine. The more exposure you have, the better.

If you want to start really small and build things up before putting money into advertising, make a simple flyer with the above mentioned information and put it on available bulletin boards in your area. Places such as grocery stores, libraries, and community centers often have a place for flyers and bulletins. Hold on to the remaining flyers. If one of your first clients is a business, ask the business owner to put your flyer in their window. If your clients are residential, leave some flyers with them to hand out to friends.

There is nothing wrong with building your business slowly, but if you want to get things started quickly, you need to rub elbows with the right people. If you are lucky, you will be in an area where there is a lot of new construction. Find your area contractors and stop by their offices to introduce yourself. Let them know you are available for painting jobs and be sure to leave a business card behind. You could also take the same approach with local interior design firms, rental companies, and real estate companies. Look on the Internet for local associations in these sectors. Contact them and ask how your business can get involved. Be sure you already have a business and contractor's license before contacting them, and let them know you are a professional and not just someone doing odd jobs.

Basic interior painting can be a lucrative way to earn money as a painter, whether you are creating your business from scratch or investing in a franchise. There are many homes, offices, and buildings, both old and new, with walls out there just waiting for your services.

The Basics of Color

"Color possesses me. It will possess me always; I know it.
That is the meaning of this happy hour. I am a painter."

~ Paul Klee (1879–1940), Swiss Painter

Color is to a painter as words are to a poet. A poet has many words to choose from, but will derive different effects and moods depending on how he or she uses them and puts them together. The same is true for your color choices. There are many to be had and many ways to use them, and each will create varying results.

Also like a poet, it is important for a painter to understand the language of color and paint. Color has a vocabulary all its own, and a painter needs to be familiar with it in order to communicate with clients and other professionals. Understanding the basics of color can help you know more about what you want at a paint store or convey ideas to clients, fellow painters, or interior decorators. If you have already had formal art training, much of the following information may be rudimentary for you, but it is always good to refresh yourself on the basics, especially if it has been a while since you were in school.

Basic Vocabulary

In the art world and in the paint store, you will hear words like "hue," "tint," and "chroma" used and you might only have a vague notion of what they mean. To find the exact color you are looking for, you need to know the difference between a "shade" and a "tint" — because they mean the exact opposite of each other. The following is a rundown of some basic color terms:

- **Hue:** An art term for color. Red, yellow, blue, and orange are all hues.

- **Value:** Refers to the lightness or darkness of a color. Every color has a value scale.

- **Shade:** The shade of a color refers to how dark the color is. Shades of a color are obtained by adding black. For example, burgundy is a shade of red, hunter is a shade of green, and rust is a shade of orange.

- **Tint:** The tint of a color refers to how light the color is. Tints are obtained by adding white.

- **Tone:** Tones of a color are achieved by adding gray. They help to "tone down" a color. It keeps colors from being too vivid.

- **Chroma:** Refers to the saturation of color or its intensity. It is color without shades, tones, or tints.

- **Monochrome:** Variations of the same color. For example, a blue monochromatic painting is comprised of various shades, tints, tones, and values of blue. It may also incorporate blue-green or blue-violet hues.

- **Primary colors:** Colors that cannot be made by mixing any other colors. They are the basis of all other colors. The primary colors are red, blue, and yellow.

- **Secondary colors:** The other three colors on the color wheel are made by mixing two of the primary colors together in equal amounts. The secondary colors are orange, green, and violet. Violet is made by mixing blue and red. Orange is made by mixing red and yellow. Green is made by mixing yellow and blue.

- Intermediate colors: Colors that fall between the primary and secondary colors on the color wheel and combine the two names. For example, red-orange, blue-green, or violet-red are all intermediate colors.

- **Complementary colors:** Colors that sit across from each other on the color wheel and have the highest contrast to each other. When they are placed next to each other, they become more intense. When they are mixed together, they will diminish in intensity and grey out. The pairs of complementary colors are red and green, yellow and purple, and blue and orange.

- **Double complementary scheme:** Using two colors that lie next to each other on the color wheel in conjunction with the two complementary adjacent colors on the wheel. For example, green and green-yellow combined with red and red-violet.

- **Split complement:** A three-color scheme made up of one color and the two adjacent colors directly opposite (or complementary) of it on the color wheel. For example, red with green-blue and green-yellow make up a split complementary color scheme.

- **Analogous colors:** The three to four colors that lie next to each other on the color wheel. For example, yellow, yellow-green, green, and blue-green together make an analogous color scheme.

- **Triads:** When talking about paint, triads are three colors that form a triangle on the color wheel. These colors work well together and have different combinations. For example, red, yellow, and blue form a primary triad.

- **Neutral hue:** Hues with a low intensity. They have an absence of any color on the spectrum and usually refer to greys. They can be warm or cool.

- **Warm colors:** The colors of the spectrum that give off a feeling of warmth. They have a fire to them. These colors include red, yellow, and orange.

- **Cool colors:** The colors of the spectrum that give off a cooler feeling. They include blue, green, and violet.

Understanding this basic vocabulary will not only help you keep up when talking about color, but it will also help you to convey your needs and ideas to clients, interior designers, and paint vendors. Plus, using these words correctly can only help you sound more intelligent and knowledgeable when dealing with these same people.

The following graphic is a visual representation of the terms tint, tone, and shade.

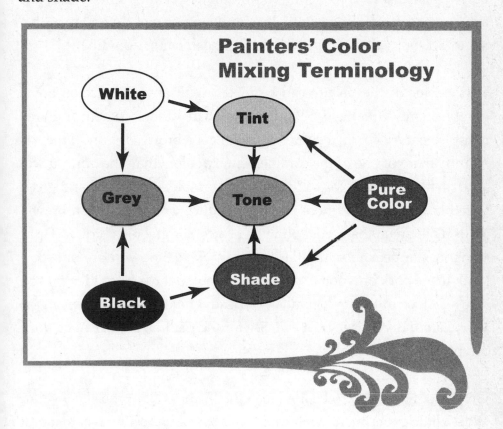

Mixing It Up

With all the possible colors out there to choose from, the option of mixing them together to make something more interesting and unique might seem a bit daunting. Basic interior painters will usually stick with the colors that come straight out of the can. This is because usually, your client will look at the paint samples on cards produced by the paint companies to make their choice. They will expect their wall to be the straight Olive Grove Green and their trim to be Vanilla Bean, because that is what they saw on the sample cards.

Faux painters and muralists will often be called upon to stretch the color spectrum to create something unique for their clients. For the artist, you can find new colors by simply experimenting. Play with a set of acrylic craft paint to see what you can come up with.

Every color in the palette can be mixed with any other color. Some combinations will have better results than others. When you mix complementary colors together, you will get a brown or grey. If there is slightly more of one of the complementary colors than the other, it will take on the neutral color's identity. For example, mixing red and green together with slightly more red will produce a warm reddish brown. With more green than red, you will get a cooler greenish brown. These variations appear in nature all the time. Next time you are out for a walk in the park or woods, see if you can pull out the color identity of a tree's bark or of the grey clouds overhead. Looking at the colors in the world around you is a great exercise for the painter, and it can be done anytime or anywhere.

Green does not have to be the green that comes out of the can or tube. With a little experimenting, it can have a more interesting feel to it or it can be more believable for the mural. First, try making green yourself by mixing yellow and blue together. This alone will give you a whole new list of greens to choose from. The green of grass in a landscape could call for more yellow in the mix in sunny spots and more blue to convey shade. You can also add various amounts of white and black to make greens that fall everywhere along the value scale. Add various amounts of grey to tone your green into a more subdued and earthy hue. But do not stop there. Go beyond the obvious to conjure up a color all its own by mixing unexpected colors to your green. Add a little orange or red and you will have a warm brownish green. Add purple or blue, you will get a more complex and cooler green. This type of mixing can be beneficial for every color you use.

Try to avoid mixing too many colors together, as this will result in a muddy hue. For more variation and interest, instead of mixing your colors together thoroughly before you use them, try laying them next to each other on your palette and dragging your brush through them both. Brush those colors together onto your wall. The result will be a combination of the colors mixed together along with streaks and flecks of each individual color standing out on its own.

When you start using paint glazes, do not miss the opportunity to create colors with depth. Glazes are a transparent or translucent paint. Different colors can be glazed on top of each other and will show the topcoat while also showing the color underneath, creating a multilayered hue. For example, lay down a glaze of yellow and let it dry. Then lay down a glaze of blue. When it dries, you will have a green with dimension. Extend this practice to the above mentioned color mixing combinations, and see what they can do as glazes rather than being mixed together before applying them to a wall.

Make It Pop

In any painting or room, there is a point of interest that can have attention directed toward it by the colors that surround the object. By putting a pure color — the point of interest — in the middle of a neutral tone, you will cause the object of pure color to stand out in contrast. Surrounding a color with white, however, will dull it because the white will be brighter. Putting a color in the middle of black or dark grey will have the opposite effect.

Contrast and directing the eye of the viewer can be achieved with more than placing neutral tones or white or black next to pure colors. Another category to look at is warm versus cool colors. The warm colors are red, orange, and yellow. These colors will appear to be in the foreground of a painting or be most dominant when placed with cool colors. Blue, green, and purple fade into the background when paired with the warm colors. These cool colors wash over distant points in a landscape and create depth.

Another way to create contrast is through value. Value is the darkness or lightness of a color. A painting with a wide range of values can create visual stimulation throughout the composition. Value contrast also helps to give objects a three dimensionality to render their form. Each pure color has its own value. You can study this by looking at black and white copies of color paintings. You will notice that yellows will appear white, purples will be black, and greens will be grey. Complementary colors — those that sit directly across from each other on the color wheel — will also create contrast when placed adjacent to one another.

Keeping It Mellow

Sometimes, less is more, especially when you are trying to create a serene or somber feel to a painting. By using slightly different values and shades of a single color, you create a monochrome painting where subtlety is the dominant factor. This also leaves room for placing emphasis on other elements of painting such as composition, pattern, shape, or movement.

High-key paintings that use values that lie at the lighter end of the value scale tend to create a sense of harmony or unity. These kind of paintings can create a serene scene, or if it is done poorly, a boring one.

Low-key paintings that use values from the darker end of the scale can create a heavy or somber feel. It might not be a good choice of scheme for rooms with little light exposure, but it can be useful if you are creating a mural with scenes of a storm or underwater.

There are also the middle-key range paintings that use values from the middle of the scale. These can also create harmony, but they can teeter on the edge of boring.

Using a limited palette can result in a pleasing painting, but it must be executed with care to avoid muddiness or overall dullness. Experiment with using just two colors. Use a set of complementary colors such as yellow and purple. Create an entire painting out of just these two colors adding only white and black. You might be surprised at how rich the result can be.

Color is the most basic tool for any painter. An interior painter can use color choices to completely transform a room into another mood or style. By painting the walls in a small room with light cool colors, painters can make the room appear larger. By covering the walls with dark warm colors, a sense of closeness and warmth will be created if needed.

With color, a muralist can be endlessly creative. Painters can unbind themselves from the conventions of color. No longer must a sun be yellow, a tree be green, or an ocean be blue. As an artist, the color choices you make can be as unique as you want or as standard as the client prefers. The possibilities with color will be an ongoing search that will make the process of painting an interesting one.

Bird mural on column. Painting by Ed Palubinskas.

Tools and Techniques for the Faux Finish

"Reality is merely an illusion, albeit a very persistent one."

~ Albert Einstein (1879–1955), Physicist

The French have dominated our artistic vocabulary. The word we use to describe a painted wall that has a look or quality that is a trick of the eye or an illusion is called "faux," which is French for "fake." By applying paint in certain ways, a plain flat piece of drywall can appear to have a sensuous texture or be made of a completely different material.

Giving walls or objects a faux finish usually takes very little time and is something that the basic interior painter and the muralist should practice doing. Providing a faux finish service with your interior painting business can only add to your ability to accommodate your clients and make you a more desirable contact for interior designers. Any muralist should be proficient at a variety of faux finishes to coordinate with their landscapes, scenes, and paintings.

While dealing with clients and making proposals, be prepared to provide your customers with a sample of what you have in mind. Interior painters provide color sample cards, which can be found at paint stores, muralists provide a preliminary sketch, so a faux painter should be able to show his or her clients a small mock piece of wall on a board in the colors and faux finish he or she is proposing. Better yet, photograph the room or object that is to be painted and feed the picture into a computer program such as 3D Home Interior Deluxe, which will allow you to insert the desired faux finish into the room or object so that the client will get a true picture of what the result will be. It will be a lot easier on both of you if the client decides he or she does not like the proposed idea at this point rather than after you have begun painting or, even worse, after the project is complete.

Tools

In faux painting, many different tools can be used to create a variety of textures, marks, and appearances. Many of the tools require little or no money to acquire. There are some common objects to keep in your bag of tricks, but tools can also be a place to use your imagination and creativity. Start looking at objects such as hairbrushes, sea shells, or even shoe soles, for their texture and ask yourself what they might do to a wet coat of paint. You might be surprised that many high end projects performed by well paid professionals are produced with things like cheesecloth, cardboard, feathers, paper towels, kitchen sponges, toothbrushes, hair combs, or newspaper. To create stamping of a simple shape, sometimes carving it into an Idaho potato is all you need. Look around you and begin playing with everyday objects to see what they can do with paint. You might just develop your own trade secret that will be disclosed to only a select few.

There are of course, the necessary items that you will need to purchase at either a home or art supply store. The list of these tools is unlimited, but the following are some of the basics:

- **A variety of brushes:** Get one of everything from the tiniest brush for detail, to the largest brush to cover big areas. Also, have a variety of flat and round brushes, as both will make a different mark or stroke.

- **Fan brushes:** These can be used in a variety of ways. They make unique fanned out marks and very thin lines. They come in a variety of sizes.

- **Sponge brushes:** These are cheap and can hold a lot of paint at one time. They come in a variety of sizes.

- **Stipple brush:** These are used for dragging techniques and distressing paint to make objects look aged.

- **Squeegee:** These come in handy for making lines into paint that are very straight and distinct.

The tools you will need are not limited to this list. This list of tools is in addition to the equipment needed for basic interior painting that is discussed in Chapter 11, such as your vehicle, ladders, and drop cloths. There are also many painters who are just starting out and prefer to buy tools and equipment as they go. If a project requires a new tool that you think you will use in the future, then that is a good time to make a purchase.

To ensure that the tools you purchase will be around for future projects, you need to take proper care of them. Paper towels can accumulate quickly if they are used to clean brushes at the end of the day. Save a few trees and use reusable rags instead. Clean them of as much paint as possible with this method. Then, using the correct solvent for the paint (paint thinner for oils and water for water-based paints), rinse them thoroughly. Wash them out with dish soap and lay them out or better yet, hang them upside down to dry. Do not leave brushes sitting in water or solvent cups, as this will warp them and cause them to lose their bristles.

When using oil paints and a paint thinner solvent such as turpentine, use metal cans or glass to hold your solvent. Most plastics will not hold up to these chemicals and will quickly melt away. When you are finished painting for the day, do not throw out the paint thinner you have been using to rinse your brushes. Instead, place it where it will not be spilled, jostled, or knocked over. After a few days, the paint will settle to the bottom, leaving behind a fresh, clear solvent to be poured into a fresh can and used again.

A Few Words on Safety

Painting is an industry that will require you to be careful with yourself, your work site, and your tools and equipment. Many paints and their solvents are flammable, and therefore, smoking should not occur anywhere near the site. When disposing of turpentine soaked rags, wet them thoroughly before putting them in the garbage, as a spark to a dry rag could cause a fire.

Turpentine and paint thinners should never be poured down the drain. Instead, follow the above tip and let the paint settle to the bottom of the container and pour the clear liquid into a reusable container. Let the sludge at the bottom dry out before putting it in the garbage.

Paint and solvent fumes can be hazardous, so ventilating your workspace is essential. Open all the doors and windows. If possible, bring fans to direct the fumes out of the room. If you have to work in an area that cannot be properly ventilated, use a respirator. To prevent absorbing chemicals into your skin while you work, wear a pair of vinyl gloves. They should be reusable and hold up well to paint thinners.

Take care of your body. Take frequent breaks to go outside, away from the paint fumes, to breathe some fresh air. While you are there, do some stretches. Your shoulders, back, arms, legs, and knees take on a lot of strain while painting. It is important to take care of these areas to avoid cramping or a tweaked back. When you are not working, do activities that will help keep your muscles strong and flexible. Try weightlifting, swimming, or rowing. Yoga is a great comprehensive practice to build strength and flexibility.

Glazing

Simple but elegant glazed panel.

Glaze is a translucent liquid that can be mixed with paint or colorant. It dries much slower than paint, which allows the painter time to work with it to create different types of fantastic finishes. There are latex and alkyd glazes that should be mixed with the according latex or alkyd paint. The general rule for mixing is one part paint with four parts glaze. Thinner mixes should be made for certain techniques such as dragging or combing or for stone faux painting.

Glazing is one type of faux finish that has many different approaches. The tools and techniques are fairly simple and with a little practice, you can become confident with them all. Buy yourself some pieces of wood that are not large but big enough for you to practice on and get a sense of what you can do on a wall. Many techniques require two or more layers of different colors to create a sense of depth.

Some basic glazing tools include:

- Rags
- Sea sponges
- Kitchen sponge
- Various sized brushes and rollers
- Hairdryer
- Sandpaper
- Steel wool

The following is a list and brief description of the various types of glazing:

- **Color washing:** This involves washing the color on with a sea sponge, rag, or even a sock. It creates soft watery colors that flow into and float on top of each other. Using earth tones gives walls an aged look, or it can be used to create a scene

Example of color washing technique. Painting by Gail Harrison.

such as a sky or underwater. Using a water-based glaze, sponge on and soften with a separate wet sponge. Work area to area, from top to bottom.

- **Dragging or striee:** This glazing technique will create a faux wood grain or fabric. Using an eggshell sheen paint, roll on a lighter base coat and let it fully dry. Then, brush or roll on a darker glaze and drag a rounded corner kitchen sponge or a dry brush over the wet glaze to remove some of the color to expose the lighter tone underneath. Do this in non-uniform strokes that are either all vertical or horizontal.

- **Ragging:** This technique is good for smaller spaces such as under the chair rail section of a wall, because it can be dramatic. This technique works well with any color sheen. First, roll on the darker-valued paint and let it fully dry. Then, completely saturate a rag in the lighter-valued glaze. Squeeze all excess glaze out and form the rag into a loose ball. Begin to dab this color on the wall

Example of ragging technique.
Painting by Gail Harrison.

while continually readjusting the rag to keep the texture non-uniform. This style of ragging is called the positive finish. There is also the negative finish that can create a softer look. Working quickly in small sections, brush on the lighter value, and before it has a chance to dry, ball up a clean dry rag and dab off the top wet layer.

- **Sponging:** This technique is similar to ragging, but it is done with a sponge. It creates a mottled look and can be layered lighter tone over the darker tone or darker over lighter for a more texturized look with more depth. It too can be used in a positive application of the top coat or a negative removal of the top coat.

- **Stippling:** This technique creates a more subtle result than ragging or sponging. It results in a suede-like appearance. Again, you can use light over dark or vice versa and make a positive application or a negative removal technique with the top coat. To do this, use a large, soft paintbrush that is applied to the wall with the tip of the brush with a stabbing motion.

- **Aging:** Creating an aged look to walls, columns, cabinetry, or furniture can be achieved through paint and glazes in a variety of ways. One of the basics is to apply a quick drying paint on top of a slow drying paint to create a crackled texture. This can be helped along with a hairdryer. Once the paint has begun to crackle, rub in an earth-toned glaze, and let it settle and accumulate into the cracks. On top of that, lightly spatter on a darker color with a toothbrush or other stiff brush.

  To create an aged look by simulating sun exposure, scrub paint off with coarse sandpaper or steel wool in areas that are more likely to be exposed, leaving the edges and corners darker.

- **Whitewashing:** This is a simple way to create an aged look by rubbing a very diluted white glaze on top of a surface that has been painted and dried. It is usually a darker color than the whitewash. Whitewashing would have little effect on a white wall.

Glazing techniques are not limited to the list above but are a boundless use of media for a variety of effects. These are some of the most basic uses of glaze, but you are always free to experiment and create new ways of creating effects.

Marbling

Faux marbling has been around for 4,000 years and began on pottery. This technique has traveled the world and has been perfected through time. Today, it is very popular with artists and clients alike. Creating the stately and timeless look of marble with paint is preferable to the high cost and strenuous labor that

Example of marbling technique. Painting by Dan and Karen Dollahon.

is involved in installing real marble, which is incredibly heavy. Putting this finish on walls, columns, furniture, or tabletops gives any object the look and feel of luxury. Using this technique for murals can come in handy when creating scenes of Tuscan landscapes or castles or for creating the above mentioned objects within the mural scene.

There are slightly different approaches to creating the marbled look. It can be achieved with water- or oil-based paints or glazes. The key to making beautiful, believable marble is to practice on scrap pieces of wood or a wall that you can paint over, until you achieve the right touch.

The following are instructions for one way to create marble on a surface:

Basic tools:

- Latex primer
- Latex paint
- Three acrylic paints in different hues of the same color: dark, medium, and light
- Polyurethane
- Mixing plate
- Sandpaper
- Paper towels
- Artist brush or feather
- Rags for cleaning brushes

Steps:

1. First, sand the surface to be marbled to rough it up and help the paint adhere. Then, clean off all dust with a wet cloth.

2. Put a layer of primer on the surface and once it has dried, apply your base coat.

3. Squirt the dark, medium, and light hues of acrylic paint onto a mixing plate and dab the sea sponge into all three. Dab and smear the colors on the wall, adding water to soften.

4. Add flowing, irregular lines or "veins" in either the darkest or lightest hue acrylic paint. It is often recommended to use the tip of a feather to make these marks, but many people use an artist's brush.

5. Apply a final coat of polyurethane for that shiny marble finish.

This is one approach to marbling, but every faux painter will have different tips, tools, and secrets to share. This is a technique that requires you to practice, experiment, and learn from others.

Graining

Graining refers to wood grain and like marbling, graining is a popular choice because it creates a stately look without the high cost. Also like marbling, there are different approaches that require some practice on your part to perfect. To create the look of wood on doors, walls, and windowsills, look into the different techniques and practice.

Example of graining technique.
Painting by Gail Harrison.

The wood graining techniques have been around for centuries and began with the ancient Egyptians. They used this technique on objects and in architectural structures, even though wood is probably not the first look that comes to mind when you picture ancient Egypt. This is probably because long ago, wood was hard to come by in Egypt because it is located in the desert where no trees grow. Before the advanced modes of trading that we have today, wood was a precious material in Egypt. To avoid the expense of importing it, Egyptians devised a way to create the look of wealth without the cost.

Today, faux graining is just as popular for the same reasons. Although it is not a precious material, wood still costs quite a bit to purchase and installation requires hard labor. Two of the most popular types of graining are mahogany and oak. Here is a description of both and the basic techniques and tools to create them.

Mahogany

This is a rich, dark, and stately wood that is used in fine furnishings, floors, doors, and trim. The following tools and techniques will allow you to give any object the look and atmosphere that this otherwise costly material creates.

Basic tools:

- Water-based glaze
- Primer
- Rusty brown eggshell paint
- Medium brown glaze
- Brushes
- Mottler (a short, soft-haired bristle brush)
- Whiting (a calcium carbonate powder mixed with water, usually used for polishing)
- Urethane
- Rags

Steps:

1. Prime your surface with two coats of primer.

2. Apply two coats of the rusty brown eggshell base color, and let it dry for about a day.

3. Apply a coat of whiting with a damp rag.

4. Mix a medium brown glaze and apply. Drag a mottler through the glaze in overlapping strokes and arcs.

5. Soften the edges with a soft, bristly brush.

6. Apply some additional glaze, and let it dry.

7. Apply a coat of urethane.

8. Repeat steps three and four.

9. Remove some of the glaze with a clean, dry brush, and after that dries, apply another coat of urethane.

Oak

Oak wood is as fine as mahogany, but with a lighter, brighter, and airy feel. The colors and tools listed below will help you create just that, while fooling any viewer into thinking it is real wood.

Basic tools:

- Water based glaze
- Primer
- Light yellow-brown glaze
- A darker brown glaze
- Clear glaze
- Brushes

Steps:

1. Prime your surface with two coats of primer.

2. Apply the yellow-brown glaze in random strokes.

3. Drag a clean brush through the wet glaze, cleaning off your brush between strokes.

4. Extend the texture by tapping the side of your brush into the glaze. Let this step dry. Depending on the humidity conditions, drying layers might need to sit overnight.

5. Apply a clear glaze, and then paint wood grain with the darker tinted glaze. It is helpful to have a piece of wood with you as a visual reference when doing this step.

6. Soften the grain lines with a brush, and let this dry.

7. Tap on a layer of dark glaze, and let it dry.

8. Apply a final coat of urethane.

Malachite

Malachite is a semi-precious stone, often put into jewelry, which is usually green and black in color with a variety of bands, waves, and striations. It has a very striking appearance that draws the eye to walls, pillars, columns, and furniture. This is a technique to practice until you feel confident in your ability to render it and offer it to a client. Look at pieces of malachite for a visual reference.

Basic tools:

- Sandpaper
- Rags
- Shellac
- Medium green paint
- Black or darkest value of green glaze
- Combs made from cardboard with non-uniform spacing between the teeth

Steps:

1. Prepare the surface by sanding off any varnish or paint, and wipe off any dust with a wet cloth. If the wood is bare, apply a coat of shellac to seal it. Let this dry.

2. Apply your medium green base coat, and allow it to dry. If you are painting in humid conditions, layers might need to dry overnight.

3. Apply another coat of shellac, and let it dry.

4. Apply an uneven coat of the black or darkest green glaze. While it is still wet, drag your combs through it with a variety of strokes such as circles, half circles, and waves. Use different combs to keep the marks from looking uniform. Allow this coat to dry.

5. Apply two to three coats of shellac.

Granite

The look of granite is great for countertops, tabletops, kitchen islands, and murals that need granite in them. It not only looks great, but it is easy and a lot of fun to do. You should be prepared to make a mess. Wear clothing that you do not mind getting paint on, and if you are working indoors, cover everything in the room with a drop cloth. It should be noted that this is not a good technique for an object that needs a smooth finish. The flecks of paint that are applied will leave a bumpy texture.

Basic tools:

- Primer
- Black or grey satin finish paint for a base coat
- Two to three different colors of satin finish paint
- A small hand-held broom for each color of paint (or use toothbrushes for smaller projects.
- Polyurethane
- Sandpaper
- Brushes or roller for base coat
- Paint tray
- Stir sticks for each color
- Feather
- Drop cloths
- Safety goggles or glasses

Steps:

1. Remove any coating of paint or varnish from the surface with sandpaper, and wipe off dust with a wet cloth.

2. When the surface is dry, apply a primer and allow it to dry. Drying time is variable due to humidity, but layers might need to dry overnight.

3. Apply a base coat of black or grey paint.

4. Dip a hand-held broom tip into a color, and shake off the excess paint. Use a stir stick to drag along the broom tip, causing it to flick specks of paint onto the surface. Use a different broom for each color, and apply them all. If you are doing a small area, use a toothbrush and your finger. It is advisable to start with the darkest color.

5. Then, drag the tip of a feather through the paint to create veins. They should be random, jagged, and not too many in number. Allow all your paint to dry.

6. Apply polyurethane in two to three coats.

Stone

Stone has a long history as a building material and an attractive accent for walls, archways, columns, and more. To create the look of stone, without all the heavy lifting and expense, using some simple steps and tools will come together to form a striking accent or a bit of photo realism within a mural.

Basic tools:

- White paint with a flat sheen
- A toned beige or taupe-like colored glaze
- A matte finish
- Foam brush
- Newspaper
- Small, thin artist's brush

Steps:

1. Properly prep your surface and apply a base coat of flat white paint. Allow to dry. Drying times may vary according to the amount of moisture in the air, but layers might need to dry overnight.

2. Apply the beige glaze with your foam brush.

3. Before the glaze dries, place a flat page of newspaper to the surface and press down with your hands with varying degrees of pressure.

4. Peel up the newspaper to see the patterns it has formed in the glaze. Some of the ink from the paper might adhere, but this can be an advantage, as it adds another natural tone or dimension.

5. Use your artist's brush and glaze to smooth out any unnatural lines or printed letters from the newspaper.

6. After the glaze has dried, apply a matte finish.

As an interior painter, muralist, or faux painter, expanding your abilities in faux painting can only mean more business for you. These techniques need practice to perfect, but for someone who loves to paint, it will all seem like playtime.

CASE STUDY: OFFERING EXTRA SERVICES

Gail Harrison
Owner and Operator of Spaces
of Beauty
Danbury, CT
gailannharrison@gmail.com
www.spacesofbeauty.com

Gail Harrison, a self-taught artist has built her business, Spaces of Beauty, by offering not just painting work but total space transformations. She sells the idea of creating a sanctuary for homes, businesses, and even gardens.

Harrison gained her basic experience for launching this business from working alongside a professional faux painter and a master gardener. Harrison now in turn extends the same opportunity to her clients by offering to let them work alongside her if they would like to learn.

Harrison began her business simply from the love and enjoyment of transforming her own home into a sanctuary. She then went to work on practicing various artistic techniques that she would implement in her services.

Harrison offers more than a painting service. She also also removes clutter, organizes spaces, and adds a touch of interior design. These extra services set her apart from other mural or faux painters in her area who offer painting only.

While creating a business, Harrison has learned a few lessons through experience. At one of her first jobs, the client expected her to move a large, heavy bed because the issue of client responsibility was not addressed in writing. She now makes sure all client responsibilities are stated within the contract.

As a good businessperson, Harrison knows her limits and does not accept jobs that are beyond what she knows she can do successfully. She turns down outdoor painting jobs or those with extremely high ceilings.

Tuscan vineyard mural. Painting by Dan Fulwiler.

Tools and Techniques for a Mural

If you are an artist and you desire to be paid for and make a living at creating works of art, then mural painting might be your ticket to the artist's life and working in an industry that you love. If you have the skills to create imagery out of paint, then you can do this.

It might be a different experience painting in a home or business rather than in your isolated studio. For one thing, you might have a constant audience while you work. Many people are fascinated with the process of painting, especially painting that creates imagery. It is one reason Bob Ross's TV show The Joy of Painting was so successful for so many years. It was watched by painters and laypeople alike. So, you might also be putting on a bit of a performance as well, and you must be — or quickly get comfortable with — being this kind of performer. If it makes you nervous to be watched, you cannot very well tell your client to go away. That would just be bad people skills and can hurt your career.

When hired to create a mural, it is your job to work with, blend in, or enhance the area in which the wall sits. You will create a piece of art that will be a semi, if not totally, permanent part of a structure. You want to make sure it will be pleasing to look at for many years. You also want to make sure it will hold up against time and wear. Often, a muralist will return for any upkeep or repair of their work, but if you are expected to do this as a part of your service, make sure it is stated in your contract with the client. If you are not willing to return, it might also be a good idea to state in your contract that your services are completed once the mural is finished. However, the best thing you can do for your client, yourself, and the mural is to determine the space's needs and use your paint, tools, and supplies accordingly. This will be the best and most proactive way to ensure that your work will outlast time and wear.

Indoor Murals

Usually, most projects will involve painting murals indoors. When painting any mural, there will be obstacles to overcome. Things like stairs, tight spaces, and high ceilings all present their own challenges. These challenges will require planning and sometimes special tools. These challenges might require the need to charge more for the extra time and equipment needed to complete the project. These extra charges should be stated in your bid and contract.

For example, not every painter has scaffolding on hand, especially the beginner. It might be necessary to rent this piece of equipment if you need to spend long periods of time at greater heights. If there is detail work to be done at the top of a high wall, scaffolding will make your time up there safer and more comfortable than teetering on top of a 20-foot ladder for long periods of time.

Extension poles and pivot tools are tools that are often used for stairwells and high ceilings. A pivot tool fits into an extension pole and allows a roller brush to turn sideways, which in turn allows you to roll paint in a side-to-side motion at out of reach heights. This tool can be handy for other places as well such as above doorways.

If you are painting on a simple low-level wall in an empty room, your needs will not be much different than painting on canvas in a studio. Some of your main concerns might be humidity, mold and mildew, exposure to chemical particles and fumes, painting surface, and light exposure.

Some rooms will be inherently humid. There is no avoiding extra humidity in a bathroom or kitchen. Some businesses might also create an extra amount of moisture in the air, such as a laundromat. If you are painting in a part of the world that is generally humid, you will want to take this into consideration as well. High-quality latex paints with a semi-gloss or high-gloss finish are the best choice for standing up against moisture in the air.

Interior walls are more susceptible to mold and mildew than walls that are exposed to fresh air and sunshine. Mold and mildew must be taken care of before creating your work of art. This should simply be a part of the cleaning process and should be the first step in prepping the wall for paint. Clean your wall with soap and water to remove any dust or dirt, but if there is a fungus on the wall, you will need something a little stronger. Create a weak bleach solution that is one part bleach to three parts water. Wipe or scrub it onto the area with a rag or cloth and allow the solution to sit for at least 15 minutes before rinsing with clean water. Never use a cleanser containing ammonia with bleach. It makes chlorine gas, which can be deadly if inhaled.

Painting and working with certain materials indoors closes people in with possible toxic fumes and particles that get released into the air. Because you will be working indoors most of the time, it is a good idea to purchase a respirator when beginning this business. To continue painting and be successful, you need to take care of your body and protect it against any hazards. Do your best when working indoors to ventilate the room. Open windows and use a fan to direct the air outside. If you are going to be painting the inside of a hospital or school, you might want to avoid using any paints or solvents that tend to be highly toxic. *To learn about the toxicity of various paints, varnishes, and strippers, as well as other hazardous materials you might encounter while on the job, and safety measures to take, refer to Chapter 10 of this book.*

Indoor mural in a child's bedroom. Painting by Shirley Fadden.

Sun exposure might not be too much of an issue when you are choosing your materials for an indoor project, but do not completely overlook this aspect. Excess exposure to light can have an effect on certain paints and colors over time. Investigate what direction the windows in the room face. If there are large windows facing the south, you need to keep excess light exposure in mind as opposed to a room with a northern exposure. The effects of light on a mural become more of an issue when painting murals outdoors.

Outdoor Murals

When you have been hired to beautify the side of a building, you might be thrilled at the chance to get some fresh air and maybe a tan, not to mention your work will be seen by more people than if it is within a structure. However, painting a mural outdoors will come with its own set of challenges and considerations. First, you will have to work around Mother Nature's schedule. If she decides to water the earth with a good rain that lasts a week, you simply have to take the week off. For this very reason, some muralists decline offers to paint outdoors.

There is also the pesky reality that you will be working with the residents of the outdoors, namely bugs. While painting outside, inevitably, a flying insect of some sort is bound to land on and get stuck in your wet paint. If you are determined to save the little creature from this fate, you might be tempted to try to free it from the wet paint, but this is a bad idea. Not only will it not survive once it has been coated with latex, but picking at your wet paint will mar your work and cause imperfections. It is best to say a little prayer for the deceased and wait for the paint to dry overnight. The next day you can come back with a wet cloth and wipe the bugs away, which should not leave too much of a mark.

Another pest you might be worried about while painting outdoors is a species known as the Urban Vandal. Because your work lives outside, it is left vulnerable to more than just the elements. In the middle of dirty, vandalized areas, a mural can be painted as an effort to beautify the neighborhood. With any luck, it will seem to have its own vandalism repellent due to its sheer purpose, which is making the inhabitants' environment a better place. Vandals tend to move on down to the unsightly overpass to spray paint their name. If you remain unconvinced, then there is a preventative measure you can take. Finish your mural with a layer of wax coating. In the event someone declares his or her love or hate for someone on top of your hard work, the wax coating, and the act of vandalism, can be removed with hot water.

As a general rule, latex paint is best for outdoor use. It holds up better against light, weather, and bonds well to masonry materials as opposed to oils that do not work well on surfaces such as concrete. When painting outdoors, you will often paint on rough masonry surfaces such as brick or concrete. When your work requires fine details or smooth finishes, create a thinner consistency with your paint. It will help your lines retain a fluid appearance, as the paint will be more successful at sinking into the pores.

When preparing and cleaning your outdoor surface, you can save yourself some work by hiring a pressure washer to do this for you. If you are going to be working on newly formed concrete, first check for the complete removal

Mural painted on brick wall of building as seen in Cambridge, Massachusetts.

of the form release agent, which is an oil or petroleum barrier used between concrete and its mold to make the form easy to remove from the cast. If it is not completely removed, your paint will quickly flake away.

When choosing the color scheme for your outdoor mural, light exposure should be a consideration. Some colors tend to fade quickly and should not be used. Paint colors with "cadmium" in the name should not be used for this very reason. Cobalt and ultramarine blue are notorious for bleaching out over time when exposed to light. Use these colors only if you mix them with a medium that holds up against light or with other colors that stay strong in the presence of the sun.

The best color choices for outdoors are:

- Titanate yellow
- Yellow ochre
- Yellow oxide
- Red oxide
- Orange oxide
- Violet oxide
- Cobalt green
- Cobalt teal
- Cobalt turquoise
- Burnt sienna
- Burnt umber
- Raw sienna
- Raw umber
- Graphite grey

- Carbon black
- Mars black
- Zinc white

Panels

There is a little secret — a short cut — for mural painters: panels. Panels are a great idea when you are asked to paint on a wall that is in bad shape. By painting your mural on panels that can be installed on top of the wall in question, you can bypass repair work and provide your client with the added feature of owning a moveable mural. Panels are something they can take along with them if they should happen to move.

Another bonus of painting on panels benefits you as the painter. By creating your work on panels, you can accept that outdoor mural job without the worry of working around weather conditions. It provides you with the ability to work in your own studio on your own schedule.

By painting on panels, you create your mural section by section and then put it all together on site. You have different choices as to what material your panels can be. Wood panels are always an option, but they can be a bit heavy for transporting. The top choice for panel material seems to be aluminum. Unlike wood, aluminum is resistant to moisture, is lightweight, and can be bent to form to different curves and corners.

Working with aluminum panels can be simple. Pieces can be cut with a jigsaw or hand saw. Make sure to sand down any edges that you cut because they are sharp and can be dangerous to you while handling. Also, when you are cutting and sanding, wear protective eyewear to guard against flying metal shavings.

Before painting on aluminum, sand the surface to give it just enough texture onto which your primer can grab. Otherwise, primer and paint will smear to thinness on a completely smooth surface.

Installing panels on site is usually done with stainless steel screws that are about 1 ½ inches in length. It is a good idea to pre-drill the holes in your panel and into the wall.

Indoor mural in a child's bedroom. Painted on canvas and installed on site. Painting by Dan and Karen Dollahon.

Look to your local metal retailer for aluminum panels or search for some on the Internet.

Another option for panels is canvas. The same rules and principles apply to this surface, which as an artist, you are probably quite familiar with.

Airbrushing

About nine out of ten muralists are going to use a paintbrush to create their art. This is good, but one way to set yourself apart is to become proficient at using an airbrush. Airbrushes are good for more than T-shirts sold at tourist shops. They can be used in fine art to create certain effects. They are the best at achieving smooth, even gradation of color, soft edges, or a haze. You can create fine lines with the airbrush by holding close to the wall when spraying or pull it farther away for wider lines. The possibilities are great when you have an airbrush on hand. Plus, they are fun to work with.

An airbrush can cost anywhere from $50 to $150 and can be found at most art supply stores or bought online. Buy paint that is specifically made for airbrushing. The difference is that the pigments in airbrush paint are ground finer so that it can move with ease through the airbrush. The choices in paints are transparent or opaque, and they come in your choice of watercolor, gauche, sign paint, or oils and acrylics, which are the best choices when airbrushing murals.

There are books and tutorials available to help the beginner learn how to use an airbrush. Look online at sites such as **www.howtoairbrush. com** or **www.airbrushartistmagazine.com**.

From Sketchpad to Wall

Once you have impressed your clients with a sketch of their project, they are going to expect to see a replica of that sketch on their wall. Transferring your small-scale sketch to a large-scale wall can be done with precision in a number of different ways.

Many artists choose to draw their sketch onto the wall freehand by simply using the sketch as a visual reference. This method works well for many skilled artists and for different styles and subject matter. If you are creating imagery that is highly stylized in your own personal way, this method would probably be fine, the average observer is not going to notice if your cartoonish flower is slightly proportionally larger than it is in your sketch. However, if you are trying to replicate a famous work of art or a portrait of someone known to the client, freehand might not be your best approach.

To make recreating a sketch onto the wall more of an exact science, many artists choose to use a grid system. Make a copy of your sketch or visual reference and measure out lines that are a certain space apart that will transfer well to the wall. For example, your sketch could have lines that are spaced one inch apart. Then, once your wall is ready to paint, make a grid on it with measuring tape and chalk with lines that are spaced one foot apart. From there, you can recreate your sketch square by square onto the wall. By breaking the image down in this way, it leaves little room for deviating from the original imagery of your sketch.

Another method that many artists choose is projecting a transfer of their sketch or images onto the wall to trace. This can be achieved in a number of ways. If you are working on a smaller scale wall, for example a 9x5-foot space, then you can photocopy your sketch onto a plastic projection sheet. Place this copy onto an overhead projector and adjust the image by zooming in and out to fit the wall. The further you zoom out to make the image larger, the fuzzier the projected lines will become. This is usually not the best method for replicating an entire scene onto a very large wall.

Some artists choose to make projections of just certain images from the sketch. They might freehand the background, but then use a projected image for a dog, a person, a car, a house, or anything that might require exact detail.

If you choose to purchase a projector, you will have a few different choices. There are the overhead projectors that are commonly seen in public school classrooms. There are also the less common opaque projectors that can project an image from a regular sheet of paper. These can be quite expensive, but you may be able to find a less expensive option at an art supply store.

Becoming a successful muralist will require technical skill, talent, and a love of art. It requires more experience and education than is needed to succeed as an interior painter or even a faux painter. Even with the tricks of tracing by projector, years of experience as an artist is a must. There are some people out there who can, on their very first try, paint a captivating image, but for most of the population, this is an acquired skill that takes time and practice. If you have a passion for creating art, the journey to becoming a skillful painter will feel like a joy ride.

When You Are Ready to Hang It Up

"Don't simply retire from something, have something to retire to."

~ Harry Emerson Fosdick (1878–1969), American Clergyman

At some point in the future, you will want to leave your business. You will either be ready to retire or you will wish to sell the business and move on. The other choices included going out of business or leaving it to your heirs. When you are ready to sell, you will know why it is important to build a profitable, saleable business. When you start your business, you should also think about your exit.

You can build a profitable painting business with a loyal customer base and an efficient business structure that will earn you top dollar when you sell. You will want to consider the fact that with a painting business, if you remain the only painter, you are the most prized asset. You will not have inventory and equipment as assets, but you will have the loyal customer base and solid business reputation that you have built for your painting business.

Exit Plan

Now is the time to develop an exit plan. You will not need as much detail for the exit plan as you needed for your business plan, but you want to develop it now and review it each year so that you can make any changes necessary. Your business situation will inevitably change from year to year, and you will want to revise your exit plan. The following are some of the basic items your plan should cover:

- **Your best-case scenario:** Do you know when you want to retire? Decide whether you want to sell the business or leave it for your family to manage.

- **Current value:** If you were to sell your business today, what is it worth?

- **Enhancing business value:** What changes would make your business more appealing for a buyer? Consider these carefully and realize that there might be some changes that you do not necessarily want to make, but that will enhance the value of the business when it is time to sell.

- **Worst-case scenario:** If you had to get out of the business today, what could be done?

- Preparing for the sale: You will want to be aware of the tax implications of the sale.

- **Leaving:** Are you in a partnership or corporation with

others, and if so, how does this affect how you leave your business?

- **Financial health for your family:** Prepare a will. Is your family trained and prepared to run the business without you?

Meet with your attorney and CPA for advice about how to create a realistic exit plan. To see some examples of exit plans, go to:

- Principal Financial Group® (**http://www.principal.com/businessowner/bus_exit.htm**)
- Family Business Experts (**www.family-business-experts.com/exit-planning.html**)

Only about 50 percent of small business owners have a business plan, and many of them plan to simply close up shop and walk away. There are other and better options for a thriving entity. If your business is doing really well, look into franchising it; although, you will still have to remain somewhat involved.

If you are a muralist, then your business will most likely be built on your name and talents. If you are no longer able to be the artist, then closing up shop is probably the best option.

Leaving Your Business to a Family Member

There are millions of large and small businesses that are operated by families. Some owners pass their business down to family members or heirs. Another option is to pass or sell the business to your business partners or employees.

There are tax implications if you leave the business to a family member. These issues include inheritance tax, trusts, and tax-free gifts. Each of these issues are complicated, and you are advised to consult with your attorney, banker, estate planner, and CPA to make sure they are handled well. More resources include:

- The U.S. Chamber of Commerce (**www.uschamber.com**)
- CCH® Business Owner's Toolkit (**www.toolkit.cch.com**)

Selling to Your Employees

You might not have family members that are interested in carrying on the business without you, so you might consider selling the business to your employees. They would need to have adequate financing, and you will want to make it a very professional transaction and include your attorney or accountant. Be aware that this can be highly emotional, as the employees buying your business might have different plans and ideas for how to "change" your business. The other issue is that it might feel uncomfortable to negotiate over money issues with friends.

Your employees might want to talk with a professional so that they clearly understand the transaction. For advice see:

- The National Center for Employee Ownership (**www.nceo. org**)
- The Beyster Institute for Entrepreneurial Ownership (**www.fed.org**)

There are many ways to handle this transaction, including transferring your business to a worker co-op or transferring directly to employees, similar to transferring it to family members, so it is a good idea to get advice and understand the process for everyone's sake.

Putting Your Business on the Market

Ask yourself exactly what it is you are selling. Take stock of what you have that is of value. It might be your successful name or simply your company's automobile, supplies, and equipment. Having decided what you are selling, document it thoroughly. Make a detailed list of what is for sale and the form in which it is being sold. You should also make sure the contract states whether you are allowed to pursue a similar competing business or solicit your old customers. Make sure this is clear in the sales contract. You never know whether you might start itching to get back in the painting business.

You can either hire an agent or a business broker or be your own agent and sell it yourself. If you decide to be your own agent, use the Internet to advertise your business and find potential buyers. If this is not an area with which you are comfortable, look to a business broker who can give insight into what your business is worth and the best way to find a buyer.

Deciding the value of your business is the hard part. Most business owners overestimate the value of their business because they do not take into account the level of risk that a purchaser would be taking by buying your business. Be realistic, flexible, and willing to negotiate.

If you have employees, let them know ahead of time about your plans to sell the business. Look out for their interests as best as you can throughout the process. They are going to be the ones who will present your business as a thriving successful business that is worth the money.

Make a detailed information package for purchasers to look at. If you are acting as your own agent, then begin advertising that your business is for sale. When you are negotiating, have some desirable aspect of your business hidden from the original proposal. By doing so, when you are trying to get the buyer to come up to your asking price, you can offer to throw something in such as extra equipment or trading stocks. You can also offer yourself as a consultant when the buyer takes over.

Expect a deposit once the contract has been signed. The money exchanged will be held by a solicitor, real estate agent, or business broker. Your contract should have details of payment requirements.

When You Have a Partner

If you are the sole owner of your business, closing shop might be easier than if you have a partner involved. Sometimes, the need to leave a business is not to retire, but because you are experiencing irreconcilable differences with your partner. If this is the case and you would like to dissolve the partnership and leave the business, then being careful and attending to details is very important. After all, like a marriage, if you have a partnership agreement, you are bound to each other by the law.

You might have a variety of reasons for wanting to leave. You might desire to simply forge your own path that your partner is not interested in, or you might be feeling like you are doing most of the work but splitting the profits evenly. Whether your reason is a pleasant one or not, following some advice before breaking up the partnership can help things end smoothly.

First, have an attorney review your partnership agreement and advise you as to your options.

Then, schedule a business talk with your partner and explain your desire to end your business relationship. Be prepared for any reaction from happy to hostile. If the conversation goes bad, maintain a professional composure. Afterward, give your partner some time to absorb the conversation that might have come as a shock.

Your options can be to discuss selling the business as a whole or selling just your share. You might even suggest that your partner buys your share out. Partnerships need to be handled delicately to prevent your relationship, and possibly your life's work, from going sour.

Leaving your life's work is a big adjustment. Whether you are happy to go or if it is something you would rather not do but must for various reasons, you need to take care of the details so there are no loose ends. Doing so can help you to move on the next phase in your life.

Faux sky painting on entryway ceiling.
Painting by Dan and Karen Dollahon. Photo by Steve Chen.

Conclusion

Painting has the power to grab ahold of a person. Sometimes, it happens at an early age, and sometimes, people succumb to its charms much later in life. Whenever it happens, those who answer the artistic call and all the possibilities it holds can also feel like painting their life away is an elusive dream.

We all have to work, and working takes up a great deal of time — too much time for someone who would rather be doing something else. If that something else is painting, then through interior painting, mural painting, and faux painting, you can become one of those lucky people who do what they love for a living. The secret, as you have learned from this book, is not usually about luck.

The secret is a mix of education and practice, with a little bit of talent and business sense. Combined, these ingredients are a recipe for a successful and happy life for a painter. With enough desire to continuously work toward success, that elusive dream is within reach. Someday, you will be able to hold that success in one hand, while holding a paintbrush in the other.

Mural in bathroom. Painting by David Kinker.

Glossary

Aging: Creating a weathered and antique look to walls, furniture, or cabinetry by stressing the surface and/or with painting techniques

Analogous colors: Three or four colors that lie next to each other on the color wheel, such as yellow, yellow-green, and green-blue

Chroma: The saturation or intensity of a color absent of tints, tones, or shades

Color wash: A technique to create a soft, watery effect with color by applying color with a sponge or rag

Complementary colors: Colors that sit opposite of each other on the color wheel, such as red and green, blue and orange, and yellow and purple

Cool colors: Colors that have a cooling and receding effect such as blue, green, and purple

Double complementary scheme: Using two colors that lie next to each other on the color wheel in conjunction with two complementary colors that lie next to each other on the color wheel, such as yellow and yellow-green with purple and red-purple

Faux: French for "fake," which is used to describe a painted surface that is meant to fool the eye

Graining: A technique in faux painting that creates the look of wood grain

Hue: Also means color; red, yellow, green, blue, orange, and purple are all hues

Intermediate colors: Colors on the color wheel that lie between a primary and secondary color and combines the two names, such as red-orange, orange-yellow, yellow-green, green-blue, blue-purple, and purple-red

Marbling: A technique in faux painting that creates the look of marble

Monochrome: Variations of the same color; for example, a green monochromatic painting consists of various shades, tones, tints, and values of green and might also have blue-green and yellow-green within the scheme

Neutral colors: Hues with low intensity and an absence of any color on the spectrum and usually refer to grays or browns

Primary colors: Colors that cannot be created by mixing other colors together, such as red, yellow, and blue

Ragging: A faux technique that creates dramatic texture by applying paint with a wadded up rag

Secondary colors: Colors that are made by mixing two primary colors, such as green, orange, and purple

Shade: Relates to how dark a color is and is created by adding various amounts of black

Split complement: A three-color scheme comprised of a color and the two adjacent colors across from it on the color wheel; for example, red with green-blue and green-yellow make up a split complement color scheme

Sponging: A faux technique that creates a mottled look by adding or removing paint with a sponge

Stippling: A faux technique that creates a subtle, suede look by adding or removing paint by tapping the tip of a brush on the surface

Tint: Refers to the lightness of a color and is created by adding various amounts of white

Tone: Tones of a color are created by adding various amounts of gray

Triad: Three colors that form a triangle on the color wheel

Trompe-l'oeil: French for "trick the eye;" a painting technique that creates the illusion of three-dimensionality and reality

Value: The lightness or darkness of a color

Vignette: A small sketch or painting with fading edges

Warm colors: Colors that create a feeling of warmth such as red, yellow, and orange

Whitewash: Creating an aged look by wiping a diluted white glaze on top of a surface

Logo painting on basketball court. Painting by Ed Palubinskas.

Author Biography

Melissa Kay Bishop was raised by a mother with a talent for drawing and painting, who took her along to painting classes and encouraged Bishop's own artwork. Bishop now holds a bachelor's of fine arts degree in watercolor and painting and a master's degree in art education. After teaching art in public schools and painting murals, she became a freelance journalist, writer, reporter, and a full-time mother to her twin boys.

Old world fresco mural. Painting by Dan and Karen Dollahon

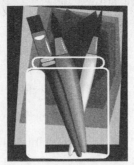

Index